NATHAN TURNER'S
AMERICAN STYLE

Classic Design & Effortless Entertaining

NATHAN TURNER'S
AMERICAN STYLE

Classic Design & Effortless Entertaining

WITH ALEXANDRIA ABRAMIAN-MOTT
FOREWORD BY INDIA HICKS

ABRAMS, NEW YORK

This book is dedicated to the women who taught me everything I know about living well—my mother, Judy, and my grandmothers, Marion and Dora.

CONTENTS

FOREWORD

I can remember clearly the first time I met Nathan. I was deeply shocked by the appalling state of his car. My children would describe it as a hobo's car—filled with clutter: empty coffee mugs, paper receipts, torn newspaper clippings, paint chips, fabric samples, odd socks, not to mention a vast, huffing Labrador retriever.

And then I toured his shop, an oasis of calm and order, rich with antique discoveries, architectural drawings, brazen photography, curated objects, and . . . a huffing Labrador retriever.

This book takes us on that tour—and beyond—to inform and delight us. Its title describes what he is best at: a sense of design that is comfortable and livable.

From decoration to dining, he is an entertainer in every sense.

India Hicks,
Harbour Island, 2012

(And if you can, drive yourself—don't get a lift.)

INTRODUCTION

HOW I DISCOVERED
MY INNER STYLE

As a born-and-bred California boy, I have lived on the coast, in the city, and in the mountains. All were completely different experiences that have impacted me in profound, distinct ways since childhood. California is such a varied place: A Northern California beach experience, for example, has little in common with what goes on at a Southern California beach. Ditto for the city and country locales. But despite all of these differences, I do see a common thread: California is, after all, the birthplace of "casual design." Seventy-five years ago, architects from all over the world came here and discovered new ways of living. The division between indoor and outdoor space became blurred. Formal rooms gave way to stunning, open areas for entertaining, relaxing, and living, and the whole notion of "relaxed style" came to be. I love that this is the one place in the world that really celebrates a barefoot, fuss-free, *and* high-style approach to living. Where else can you get that?

It's such a unique mix, and my approach to decorating and entertaining is all about finding new ways to live and celebrate with low effort and high style—whether you live near the beach, in the city, or in the country. Now more than ever, with so many of us leading hectic lives, I feel that stuffy, high-maintenance living is simply a thing of the past. Who wants to slave over a meal all day when there are one hundred other items on their to-do list? Or create a living room that's overdecorated to the point of needing a "Keep Out" sign? It might have made sense a few generations ago, but it doesn't now that everyone seems to have less time and more to do. That said, living well is still an absolute necessity. My goal is to create a new era of laid-back, highly stylish design and entertaining ideas that can be implemented without huge amounts of effort or expense. Whether you're looking to redesign just a small room or the entire house, or whether you want to throw an intimate dinner party or a major blowout, I'm convinced that it can be done without going into debt, and while having a great time!

At home in Malibu with dogs Daisy and Nacho. The flag photograph is by Oberto Gili.

THE LITTLE SHOP THAT COULD

ABOVE: Right from the start, my shop became my own personal "decorating lab," with finds like this pair of antique architectural French lamps.

OPPOSITE: At the shop, Daisy lounges on a nineteenth-century English sofa in front of an eighteenth-century Italian screen hung with a mix of modern prints and antique oil paintings.

When I opened my store in Los Angeles almost exactly ten years ago, I honestly had no idea where it would take me. None. Back in 2002, I was totally new to L.A., had very few contacts in the design world, and barely had any friends in the city! But what I did know was that I was determined to open a space that was more than a shop, that could be shared with others and used to explore different ways of entertaining. To this day, all of these years later, I continue to think of my store as something of a laboratory where I'm free to experiment with paint, furniture, art, and accessories for everything from intimate cocktail gatherings to full-blown mega parties where the valet line wraps around the block.

Back when I was just starting out, I tried to stay focused on the process, not on the outcome. There were days in the beginning when not a single customer would come in, but I'd keep myself busy by moving things around or doing some kind of outreach in the design community. I stayed with the process, which is a good thing, because if I had obsessed over becoming successful, I probably would have given up a long time ago! This approach stays with me, and I still do my best to be laser-focused on what I love: creating stylish and functional spaces, and low-effort, high-style entertaining.

Back in 2002, however, I hadn't yet fully explored this passion. At that point, I was just looking for a space that would make for a good design location in L.A.'s highly competitive world of home showrooms. Then, one day while driving around town, I discovered a tiny street called Almont Drive. It's in West Hollywood, sandwiched between the heart of Santa Monica Boulevard, with all of its bustling restaurants and clubs, and Melrose Avenue, which is where a lot of the high-end L.A. home showrooms are located. Almont Drive was a small and quiet street with practically no retail action. It was there that I found a shabby bungalow with overgrown trees and a handwritten sublet sign. The bungalow was completely scruffy, and yet something compelled me to call the next day. Cut to a month later, and I had opened my first store.

It turns out that how I got from that forlorn and forgotten place to a shop that had my name on the awning involved a process that I would replicate over and over and over again. The shop ended up being just one of many projects where budget, time, and space would create unique decorating challenges requiring stylish and clever solutions. As it is for any person approaching a new business venture, the name of the game was to keep overhead low. I definitely wasn't in a position to call in an architect and overhaul the place with fancy, brand-new everything. Instead, I had to take this 1930s bungalow, with its series of tiny rooms, its less-than-perfect finishes, and its overgrown garden, and make the best of it with the least amount of money. Yes, the architectural bones were there, but so was an enormous amount of work.

Since I needed to make the place look amazing for as little money as possible, I used the old standard cheap-and-chic trick: I painted all of the rooms a single neutral color (Behr's "Windsor Castle"), which went on the walls, trims, moldings, and doors to make them sort of disappear. It's a great approach for any space with less-than-ideal finishes. Then I put seagrass on the floor, my never-fail trick for giving a space an instant lift in the elegance department without spending a ton of money. The paint and floor coverings helped draw the eye away from the space's imperfections and instead put the focus on its cottage-like proportions, the cozy fireplace, and of course, all of the furniture, art, and accessories that I was going to put in each and every room.

I can't stress how much I didn't know, when I was first beginning, about opening up a store, much less creating an interior design space that would appeal to the city's top decorators. Call it the original trial-and-error laboratory test. (Emphasis on error, because there were lots of them.) But, along the way, I learned everything I needed to know about my own version of decorating and entertaining.

GETTING THE PARTY STARTED

I know that entertaining can be stressful. Among the many worries is "Will anyone show up?" In the early days of the shop, sometimes it'd just be me and my cousin. No joke! Other times, the store would be filled to capacity. I think the key to successful party throwing, whether you're doing it professionally or personally, is to focus on the process, not the outcome. Sometimes parties work out and sometimes they don't. The important thing to remember is that it's one of the best ways to spend time with people and share a moment.

The shop has all the comfort of home, including this settee that I upholstered with antique suzani cloth.

My original store had an entry area, a dining area, a living room–type space, and even a kitchen that I installed. When I opened it, it was a simple yet hardworking space tucked into the back of the shop; I never imagined just how much use it would get! Within the rooms were many smaller nooks and alcoves that required their own thoughtful vignettes. I got good at creating those "design moments," as they're referred to. It became second nature. When someone would come into the shop and buy half a room's worth of stuff, I'd suddenly have to reassemble the entire puzzle and make different vignettes. It was a passion—as was mixing unexpected items together. Because I started out as a retailer, not as a designer's assistant, I think I had the mental freedom to really let myself experiment. I mixed things up because I didn't know differently. I played with combinations of new and old, traditional and modern, patterned and plain. My lack of experience gave me the courage to put all of these crazy things together. Did it always work? Definitely not. But when it did, I would remember it. And I slowly started building a sense of confidence about my own particular style. That's something I always encourage people to do: Don't run out the door and start buying things. First begin with moving things around. See what works. Don't get stuck with the idea that the entire room will fall apart unless *this* framed photo spends the rest of its life on *that* end table, or *this* armchair is placed in *that* corner. Play! Experiment. Have fun. See what works. You'll start to develop an eye and then when you do go out and make purchases, they will be far more informed.

I experimented the same way with color. I was constantly repainting the walls in my showroom. Whether I was inspired by a change in the season, or just kind of in the mood for something different, I was rarely without a can of paint at the ready. I'd put a bold violet on the wall and discover that it not only worked, but it made a space come alive and looked gorgeous against more neutrally colored antiques. Or I'd paint a back wall orange, hate it, and then have to spend the night frantically painting over it before the next day. These experiments taught me that if you want to give spaces those big moments of color, you need to pare everything else down. Those are the kinds of design lessons that gradually emerged. And I'm still convinced that for anyone who wants to change things up in their home, paint is the absolute most affordable and forgiving friend. When it comes to paint, I say just go for it.

THE ULTIMATE BLANK CANVAS

My shop became my set, in a way, a place where I was free to experiment with all kinds of decorating styles depending on the season, the inventory, or my mood. And believe it or not, from my West Hollywood location, one day I would decide to make it an English country cottage and start filling it with wildflowers, old leather club chairs, oil paintings, and fabulously faded floral throw pillows. Another day, I might have decided that we were taking the store in a nautical direction. Out would come the shells and the coral and the bleached-wood garden furniture. And still other days I'd merely treat it as what it was: a cozy home store located in the middle of a bustling city. My point is that you decide what kind of home you want to live in; the architecture doesn't decide for you, and neither does your location (within reason). I love that sense of freedom and finding the ability to incorporate different looks and styles.

Perfect matches need not apply at my shop. Here, a colorful screen made from vintage suzani cloths keeps company with a collection of antique French wine jugs. The flower painting is by Verónica Navajas.

During my first few years of owning the shop, I learned just as much about entertaining as I did about retail. A decade ago, the concept of throwing a dinner party in an antiques store was a total novelty in L.A. Then the *Los Angeles Times* caught wind of what I was doing and they came out to cover a small get-together that I put on at the shop for six friends. Keep in mind, I wasn't Mr. Popular in town at this point; designers weren't banging down my door. But with just a few good friends and some simple but well-prepared food, my concept of casual and stylish entertaining started to come into focus. And then all of a sudden, my idea of a low-key get-together surrounded by beautiful antiques made the cover of the *Los Angeles Times*. Voilà, I had an audience. And over time, my client base and passion for great design continued to evolve and grow. That was my start: equal parts passion, hard work, and a certain amount of luck.

Today, I have a new store on Melrose Avenue. I call it my big-boy shop. The area has much more traffic, and the store has a higher profile. Now, unlike before, I don't know everyone who walks in the door. But that's OK. I wanted to continue growing my shop and my business, which meant leaving my cozy cottage and moving to a location where I'm now wedged between Rose Tarlow and Waterworks, two of the biggest companies in the decorating business. But even though this location is much fancier, I still think of the smaller shop as my second home—or maybe even my first. Everything is still completely hands-on; I do all of the purchasing and styling myself, and, on any given week, it's not uncommon for me to spend more time in the shop than at home.

OPPOSITE: Shop by day, entertain by night: Serving dinner in the store is one of the best parts of having a shop! For this dinner party, I used eighteenth-century Swedish chairs to surround a table that's covered with a custom-made check tablecloth. Yes, sometimes wine spills on the merchandise. We deal.

THIS PAGE: A set of four antique French lamps stands in front of American artist Kevin Paulsen's painting.

ABOVE: The Big Mix-Up: A German botanical drawing rests against an eighteenth-century Tuscan cupboard.

ABOVE: I love introducing a really organic element into a space, no matter how "formal" it's supposed to be. Here in the shop, I set that element atop an eighteenth-century Spanish coffer with Grand Tour photographs and an Italian fresco.

OPPOSITE: A working fireplace in the shop made all the difference in the world in terms of creating a homelike environment. Here, I paired a Nathan Turner for Elite Leather Harnell Sofa with a Nathan Turner for Elite Leather Timms Coffee Table.

PART ONE

GOING COASTAL:
Laid-Back
Beach Chic

GROWING UP WITH THE SEA

ABOVE: High seas! *The Bolero*, my family sailboat, tooling around San Francisco Bay.

OPPOSITE: My passion for blue and white started young. Here I am on the beaches of Puerto Vallarta at seven years old. Check out my waterproof camera and cocktail! (Don't worry—it's just guava juice.)

WATCHING WAVES IS ONE OF THE CLOSEST THINGS TO INSTANT happiness that I know. I grew up in Northern California, in the East Bay of San Francisco, and I was lucky to have a childhood that involved lots of time at the beach all throughout the year. Weekends were usually spent on our sailboat, *The Bolero*. We'd tool around the bay near home, or go up north to Point Reyes and Tomales Bay. There'd be clamming and digging for oysters—more of what you'd think of as a Maine experience, as opposed to a California one—where we were usually in windbreakers and rain boots with those dramatic rocky bluffs in the background.

In the summer we would go to Stinson Beach, a great stretch of "real beach" in the Bay Area, or head to Mexico and spend time in Puerto Vallarta, which couldn't be more different from the steep cliffs on Northern California's coastline. For me, going down there was a tropical adventure with *palapas*, lots of fresh fruit juices, and big, vibrant colors everywhere I looked.

But it wasn't until I was a teenager, when my mom bought a house in Laguna Beach, that my love affair with Southern California and its one-of-a-kind beaches began. My passion for this kind of classic *beachy-beach*—its wide swaths of sand, smell of suntan oil, and volleyball games—was immediate and overwhelming. And P.S., it isn't that common for Northern Californians, who fancy themselves more sophisticated and cultured, to fall in love with Southern California. But at age seventeen, all I knew was that Southern California was warm and beautiful, and once we drove down to our place in Laguna Beach—a 1920s bungalow plopped right on the sand—we practically never had to get in the car again all summer.

I didn't know it then, but during those summers in Laguna Beach, something was crystallizing in me. It was the notion of beach living—Southern California style—a world where things could be laid back *and* amazingly comfortable *and* incomparably beautiful. It was a new revelation for me that my parents' bungalow—which, even as a teenager, I insisted they paint white-white and fill with colorful, comfy furniture—could have sand on the floor, wet towels everywhere, not a precious object in sight, and *still* be drop-dead. And today, that same notion continues to inform my version of beach chic and my commitment to keeping it unfussy, fun, and stylish.

THE RULES:
GOING NATE-IVE AT THE BEACH!

1. Rely mostly on relaxed fabrics, preferably washable, wearable, and no-fuss. (Hint: Outdoor fabrics work incredibly well.) The whole point of being at the beach is that it's one of the world's most relaxed environments. You don't want to be on pins and needles about ruining some fancy silk ottoman! Expect sand in the house. (Maybe even invite it!)

2. Work to loosen the line between inside and out. Put an indoor dining set outside, use outdoor chairs inside, rely on garden accessories for interiors—mix it all up for a feeling of instant, laid-back style.

3. Invite in an abundance of natural elements: Think wicker, driftwood, grass cloth, and matchstick blinds. Unfinished textures work amazingly well in beach homes, and they instantly force spaces to feel more relaxed.

4. Blue and white may be the obvious color palette, but don't shy away from them because they're tried and true. After all, those are the colors of the sea and clouds! But you don't have to get into a clichéd decorating rut. You can punch up the blue-and-white scheme by adding other colors in small ways that create a big impact, making a classic and expected beach look all your own.

PARADISE FOUND
(AND THEN TOTALLY REDECORATED)

When I first walked into this Malibu beach cottage, it was all shag carpeting, orange-colored walls that made zero sense, and really depressing furniture. It was so dark and dreary on the inside, but it didn't even matter. My partner, Eric Hughes, and I knew it was *the* place the minute we stepped in. It was perfect: a small, wood-framed beach cottage from the 1930s with insane views of the Pacific Ocean. This is as uninterrupted as views get, and when the tide is high, the water goes *under* the house. That is when this place really feels like a boat—cozy, snug, and exactly what we wanted. It completely takes me back to my sailing days, and that idea of creating a houseboat experience really appealed to me. Here's how we got from dark and dreary "beach bastardized" to what I'm now calling Modern Nautical.

ABOVE: Eric and me at home in Malibu.

OPPOSITE: Keeping things relaxed and beautiful is the sweet spot of design, and I think this little moment with a vintage American flag and a Pottery Barn console captures that in a perfectly beachy-chic way.

BLENDED STYLES

Full confession: Eric and I are not exactly what you would call decorating soul mates. He's the guy who has about five prized possessions; I'm the person with about 500,000 things. His style is stark and beautiful; mine is cozier, full of more things. (I didn't say "cluttered," but Eric might accuse me of that!) This was our first place together so I thought, "This could be amazing or this could totally be the end of our relationship." But the one thing we were able to agree on was that we both like small spaces. That is key. Although I often decorate big, rambling houses for clients, neither of us wants that for our home. After a certain point, you can only use so many rooms. Beyond that I feel like you lose the sense of coziness that's so appealing to me. Unused rooms just feel so cold. So many people are so focused on square footage, which at the beach almost inevitably costs top dollar. But I say, when it comes to the ultimate coastal experience, focus less on the size of the house and more on the quality of its location. At less than 1,800 square feet, this home is more like a huge shack—and we use every square inch of it.

If I want vast, I go outside. And here at the beach, I'd rather be outside most of the time anyway. We have the whole Pacific Ocean out there and a deck that's roomy enough to host a dinner party. But when it came to dealing with how we were going to decorate the inside of the house, that's where Eric and I both had to give in to the other person's style a bit. Working in our favor was the fact that Eric, having lived in Malibu while attending college, is as much a beach person as I am. And we both had this notion of creating a place that would feel Modern Nautical—to us that meant cozy yet airy and filled with lots of light. The house also had to be highly functional. We have two dogs, and all four of us are always coming in straight from the beach, so there's usually sand everywhere. We wanted something that would look beautiful but never feel precious. The key to happy beach living: Stay away from anything precious. Give in to the fact that sand is going to get into the house and that wet towels are going to be left outside. Opt for durable fabrics and low-maintenance materials, so that you can focus on enjoying the beach, not maintaining some kind of coastal museum!

CREATING A RELAXED CANVAS

We started with Benjamin Moore's "Super White" in a gloss. True, I don't usually go for a glossy finish, but when you're trying to create that super-clean boat vibe, the shiny surface that a glossy paint gives strikes just the right note. And it is also incredibly easy to clean.

Next we replaced that shag carpeting with wall-to-wall seagrass, which instantly lightened up the space and made it feel really clean. I always encourage people to use seagrass when they're looking to cover large areas of flooring affordably and elegantly. It never fails!

After we created the backdrop, then came the fun part: pulling in lots (well, not *tons*, after all, Eric was working on this project, too) of stuff.

When starting any project, it's key to decide on your colors before you let anything into the room. I always work that way. Trust me—you will save so much money and prevent so many headaches if you work this out ahead of time. We knew for this house that we wanted blue, white, and natural elements. OK, so those are obvious choices when you're working on a beach house, but there are so many innovative and fresh ways to do blue and white that don't look like a bad Old Spice ad. Three colors are enough to start any project. With more, things can start looking a little frenetic; less and they can go too sterile. Also keep in mind that white, natural tones, and blue just represented my main template for color. Of course we added in other colors here and there as accents. But the big statements stayed within those three colors. Stick with that and you'll have a space that is both visually balanced and lively.

With the color palette in place, we then started looking for stuff that we love: furniture, fabrics, art, and lighting. And, yes, this was the part where I wanted to load up every inch of the space and Eric wanted to keep it stark. There was plenty of push and pull, but in the end, I think we got something that neither of us could have accomplished on our own, and for that I especially love this home.

STACK IT!

Here's a secret to living well in small spaces: Get stackable chairs that are stylish enough to be left out. I use Pottery Barn's Tolix Café Chair. They're gorgeous, feel solid and not flimsy, and are easy to move from our dining room to the deck, depending on where we're eating or entertaining. When we don't have people over, Eric and I just store all six of them in the closet, where they don't take up very much space.

INSPIRATION & INGENUITY

We wanted to make our own sort of beach statement that people would feel the minute they walked into our house, one that would feel relaxed and functional and not fancy. One of the keys to creating a beautiful beach atmosphere is to stay away from anything that feels formal: Avoid overly tailored furniture and stay away from heavy finishes. With that in mind, we wanted to create an entryway that would immediately evoke this relaxed, highly functional vibe. First, Eric had the idea of using a wooden coatrack. It's super simple, something we bought online for about seventy dollars but customized so it didn't look like something off-the-shelf. We painted it the same shade of Benjamin Moore white to blend in (although it could look really cool in a contrasting color as well).

Then I set about hanging stuff on the coatrack that we actually use: towels, bathing suits, and hats. While completely functional, I also wanted this to look like art, so I thought about it carefully and took my time in placing things. True confession: The towels are Hermès—I love those bright colors. I think people get caught up in the idea that creating vignettes like this is pretentious, or a waste of time because it's all going to change at some point. Not so! Give yourself permission to make beautiful little arrangements throughout your home. I don't know of a better mood lifter than to see something at home that's been beautifully, thoughtfully arranged. And here's the real trick of it all: Everyday objects can make just as beautiful a statement as luxury ones. Aside from the Hermès towels, everything here is super basic, including my map collection that I hung all around the edges. They look great grouped, but these are just maps I collected that aren't precious or expensive. Some I even picked up at tourist kiosks, and one I got from a Baja California gas station. I unified the grouping by putting them in unfinished wood frames. (You could also do the same treatment with postcards, kids' art, or almost anything!) But all along I knew this little "design moment" that I was creating in the entryway could totally turn into a cluttered creep show if I didn't really edit what I let into the space. So I took the time to curate all of this carefully so that it fit together. Yes, it's edited, and yes, I took some time putting it all together, but it gets used almost daily and is so much cheaper than cabinetry!

Lulu DK and India Hicks are the queens of the beach for me, so I wanted to incorporate a bit of both of them into this house. I love Lulu's fabrics; they're so gorgeous. And India, to me, is a genius at bringing in that beach vibe in a relaxed and effortless sort of way.

I love this entrance area to our Malibu house. It's both beautiful and completely functional. We use everything at this house. Here, the area is both the entrance and the dining area when it's too cold to eat outside on the deck.

Unexpected items like Oberto Gili's "Goldfish" photo are combined with more on-the-nose seafaring stuff like this vintage naval chain. I love that mix.

Let's face it: A lot of fabrics aren't cheap, so I used higher-price textiles in small but impactful ways. And that's an important design lesson: If you're really in love with a certain textile that is expensive, don't just assume you can't use it. Even a single yard can go a long way. Make a single throw pillow out of it to star on your sofa, then cast other more affordable pillows to support your prized piece of material.

When it comes to upholstering the seating and doing the window treatments—the places where you really rack up the yardage—the trick is to go for extremely affordable options. Drapery and upholstery can eat up your budget faster than almost anything else, so you need to stay focused on the less expensive options when you're using this much yardage. We went with super-affordable options, mostly because it's just not my style to spend a ton of money on my own home. Yes, I will spend money on some nice things, but I don't think every single purchase has to be that big-ticket item. Here's the truth: Most of the big things in our beach house weren't pricey, and some of my very favorite things barely cost anything. When I'm at the beach with my dogs, with sand on my feet and wet towels everywhere, it would be impossible for me to enjoy myself if I were worrying about furniture upholstered in fabric that cost $150 per yard.

BATTEN'D UP!

We used wood batten board in the living room. I love it because it adds some architectural interest to the room in an unpretentious way that reinforces the coastal vibe. But here's the secret: Carry the board all the way up onto the ceiling. It finishes off a room with a custom look that seems way more expensive than it is. It's just inexpensive board that you can get at Home Depot. Nothing fancy.

ODE TO INDIA

One of my ultimate style mentors is India Hicks. Here I am hanging out (literally!) at her home in the Bahamas. She's a master at creating the ultimate chic-but-super-laid-back lifestyle. I've been to her place several times, and I am always discovering something new. I'll pick up a tip and end up bringing another one of her ideas to my own home.

This isn't so much a case of design inspiration as much as deliberately copying India Hicks. But I encourage this kind of design piracy! If you see something you love, do it! In her stunning home in the Bahamas, India took a printer's box for hot-metal type and filled each little area with shells that she collected. I loved it so much that I emulated my own version in the bathroom with an old box (purchased on eBay) that I filled with some of my favorite shells.

I clock a lot of hours on this sofa. It's my Nathan Turner for Elite Leather Spencer Sofa that's slipcovered in super-affordable and durable duck cloth. You just sink into it and never want to get out. The basketweave light fixture is from Pottery Barn.

So I opted for things like the Spencer Sofa I designed for Elite Leather. I thought it really married both my and Eric's styles. It has clean lines and a mattress seat that makes it comfy and cozy. (Confession: As much as I love being outside, there are also lots of foggy days in Malibu when all I do is lie under a big blanket and watch movies.) I wanted this sofa to be as comfortable and cozy as possible, so we slipcovered it in a heavy duck cloth in navy. The fabric is about twenty dollars a yard and the easiest thing to just put in the washing machine when it gets dirty. I don't have to worry about it. We also opted for Ikea curtains, which again, are insanely affordable. But they're also exactly what we wanted. What could be more beachy than white canvas drapes with those huge metal grommets? They let in tons of light, and canvas is easy to wash.

Once those basic whites, naturals, and blues were in place, then it was time to have some fun. Eric and I layered a blue and orange dhurrie rug on top of the seagrass carpeting to bring some pattern and color into the living room. Then we set about making simple, underdecorated moments throughout the main areas. One of my favorites is a crazy chain sculpture that goes from the floor to the ceiling. That was Eric's find, and what I love about it is that it ties into that whole nautical boat-chain thing, but the really rustic unfinished wood keeps it from going too literal. Consider these kinds of quirky, unexpected pieces—they could be sculpture, art, or even furniture—to take beach décor out of the expected realm and into a more unique place. You really only need one or two pieces like this in a room to give it a little bit of modern edge and a lot of personality. And it's far more effective than a captain's steering wheel!

BULLETIN BOARD 2.0

We wanted a bulletin board in the living room, but I think they can look really dinky and cheesy when they're small. So we decided to go DIY and build an oversized board that would make a huge statement. This is actually the cheapest bulletin board I could find. It's a six-footer that I got at Staples and took to my framer, who installed a chic, wide, glossy frame on it. The frame immediately made it look super custom. And it also made it appropriate to fill such a huge wall.

When decorating bedrooms for couples, I always try to take both styles into account. It may seem like an impossible task if one of you is a strict traditionalist and the other is a committed modernist, but I think our bedroom proves that two styles can come together to create something fresh, unexpected, and totally personal. Here, we tucked our bed into that little cutout in the wall and then it was Eric's idea to add that fiberglass marlin for a little whimsy. We had it lacquered a deep navy blue to get it away from feeling somewhat cheesy and make it read more like a modern nod to the sea. It even came with little tabs on the back that made hanging it really easy. Would I have put that marlin up there? No way! Nor would I have chosen those lights from CB2 (that were under thirty dollars each!). I would have picked something more rustic, maybe even antique, but Eric loved these very modern, stainless-steel fixtures. And once we put it all together—the shiny white walls, the crazy marlin, and those industrial-looking lights with that great whimsical headboard fabric—it perfectly captured the sense of Modern Nautical that we were going for. The design lesson: Mix it up! Let both people have their most beloved elements in the room and connect it all with color. The result will often be a combination that takes things out of the predictable realm and into totally stylish and original territory.

OPPOSITE: For this little writing area in our bedroom, I framed a vintage flag-inspired scarf and hung it above a nineteenth-century English writing table and a French farm chair.

ABOVE: Lulu DK's Sunshine fabric is on the headboard, but I didn't need a ton of yardage, and I'll never get tired of it. A vintage French naval wool blanket gives a touch of beachy chic without going too literal.

REUSE!

Custom headboards can totally break the budget, so here I took a decorating shortcut to save money. Using my mom's old headboard from our Laguna Beach house, I had this slip-cover made that basically fits right over it. It's totally repurposed, and I love the fact that I'm reusing something from my childhood in a new way.

Even the bookcase gets the batten-board treatment.

A COLORFUL BEACH HOUSE

When I first walked into this home, I was like, "This is easy. I'm going to paint everything white and we'll sort of replicate my beach house." And then I went back and took a closer look at its architecture and materials and realized, "Oooh, I can't do that. I need to really analyze this house and go with what is here."

And what was there was one of those classic L.A. mid-century case-study homes. It's all about ninety-degree angles, huge windows, and somewhat low ceilings. I used to be terrified of decorating these kinds of places. I'd just think of those austere case homes with the awful, low vinyl sofas that you could never get comfortable on—my mental image was of a 1960s dentist's office. But then I had a lightbulb moment that has stayed with me ever since: You don't need to let architecture determine everything. This is so important to remember, because whether you rent or own, odds are you don't live in a custom-built home. You have to adjust to the architecture that you inherited. But you don't have to be dominated by it. That was the lesson here. Just because this was a mid-century house didn't mean I had to design within that school of thought. I could acknowledge it, which I did, but I didn't have to be beholden to it. For me, this meant that I could inject color, fun, and comfort into the home's specific kind of architecture. The clients were two young, creative people from New York City who wanted a fun and vibrant Malibu experience. So the project became all about how to make this place lively, and the notion of working with a lot of color became the focal point.

ABOVE: For this client's house, I put a really rustic-looking, reclaimed-wood table atop a fluffy Flokati rug. The collection of vintage California pottery completes the look without anything getting too precious.

OPPOSITE: For this huge sofa set, I went with a really bold Lulu DK fabric called Colors. It just makes such a cheerful statement. The large floral acrylic is by Verónica Navajas.

MAKING A CASE FOR COLOR

So it may look like this living room has huge amounts of color (yes, there are some big doses of it), but I really concentrated the bold tones on just a few pieces, then balanced out all those oranges and blues and greens with other more natural elements to keep it all from looking like a jelly-bean factory.

The starting point for the entire living room is that fabric from Lulu DK (yes, I'm a little obsessed with her textiles, if you haven't noticed by now) that I used on the shell of the sofas. I liked it because it had all of those great color choices: cheerful and bright oranges, greens, and blues. Let's face it: The pattern is busy, which is why I decided to do the cushions in solids. If I made the entire sofa in that print, I would have had one of those Gloria Vanderbilt–type situations where you do the walls and curtains and then a jumpsuit all in the same crazy pattern! This is a great way to bring in a bold print without overwhelming a space. Just use the pattern on the shells of seating, then do the back and seat cushions in a solid. I love that. You could so easily use a stripe or a floral for the same effect.

These huge expanses of glass might tempt some people to go with a fancy window treatment. But here anything that takes away from the view is a mistake. I went with unfinished matchstick blinds to keep the living room simple and beachy.

To me, orange is that ultimate neutral color. It's like the Switzerland of the color wheel—not too masculine or too feminine—and it's great for couples. So I chose that hot, cheerful tangerine for the sofa cushions, but to do both sofas in the same color would have been too much of the same, so we did the other sofa in a lighter blue.

Here, we have this blast of all of this crazy color on the seating in the living room—and that's enough. Remember that: If you love bold color, go for it, but you only need a couple hits of it. Then the key is dialing all of the other elements way down to neutral territory. So this room was about using color, and then framing it in a way that balanced it all out. To achieve this I did seagrass on the floors and added that Flokati rug, which is to me the quintessential California floor covering: beachy, comfy, cozy, and so soft. A driftwood coffee table has just a few objects on it, none of them bursting with color, all pretty organic in feeling. The window treatments are just unfinished matchstick blinds, a cheap and cheerful solution from Blinds.com and totally appropriate for the era and style of the house. I skipped color entirely in the dining room and went with all natural pieces like the coconut bead chandeliers, wicker chairs from Pottery Barn, and a bamboo dining table.

ARTFUL ARRANGEMENTS

In a room this colorful, the last thing you need is a vase of red tulips to take it over the edge. So when you're looking to do florals or centerpieces in these kinds of high-color spaces, opt for natural items: Put agaves or palm fronds or something like that in a vase to keep it all fresh but not overloaded with color.

I covered the fireplace wall in grass cloth because I love the material. It's affordable and appropriate to this era of home. If your house is lacking architectural detailing or in need of some texture, grass cloth is one of the best ways to get a tactile, interesting look without spending a ton of money. Here, the cloth ended up framing the fireplace in a way that elevated and updated it beyond its funky '60s vibe. The rest of the walls are all Benjamin Moore's "Super White" (flat, not glossy). If I had added color to the walls, this would have looked like a clown house. But instead, the home is able to project the earthy, natural California moment that I wanted to bring in.

OPPOSITE: I love hanging art salon style in a non-fussy way. To keep it even more laid-back, I leaned some art against the wall.

ABOVE LEFT: I left the original mid-century fireplace just as I found it but gave the setting a pop of brightness with a colorful vintage print.

ABOVE RIGHT: Why battle with one of the world's greatest views of Malibu? A mid-century Danish chair from Leif Antiques paired with a rope sidetable fills this corner without over doing it.

BOOKSHELF STYLING 101

This is one of the top problems I see with clients: how to style those darn bookshelves! Here are the rules: You either go all books, arranged by similar height or you combine books and objects, which can be anything but not (repeat, not) framed photos, which always look better on a vertical, not horizontal, surface. (And, yes, that includes the grand piano! It just looks better to have photos on walls instead of tables, instruments, etc. Very few exceptions apply to this rule.) Here, I took two simple West Elm Parsons bookshelves and let the contents stand out. It's all about balancing the open spaces and filling them with interesting objects. Also, change the direction of books: some stacked, others standing. And don't forget to weigh the bottom shelf down with a solid row of books.

SUNSET INSPIRATION

One afternoon I was home just as the sun was setting, and the client called and said, "Look at the sunset! That's what I want my bedroom to look like." So I went out on my deck and saw that it really was unbelievable. There were lilacs and purples with these bright bursts of yellow. I got all excited about it, but then I went and started pulling fabrics together and I thought, "This is insane! It's way too much!" I've never mixed purples and yellows together before. So I pulled back on the idea of giving each of those colors equal billing and decided to cast that insane sunburst curtain fabric (yes, Lulu DK!) as the star of the room and painted the walls a super pale yellow. The purples and lilacs then became supporting colors that would accent the yellows. And it's an important lesson to keep in mind: When you're using two strong, competing colors in a room, cast one as the star and the other as the supporting tone. Otherwise you'll get a clash of color egos!

BEDROOM POLITICS

I realize that this is a pretty feminine color palette for a bedroom, and keeping in mind that I didn't want to alienate the husband, I decided to use extremely clean-lined, mostly vintage furniture, some of it verging on austere. This balances out all the color, and it's a trick that can be applied to any space. If I had put a four-poster bed in here with these kinds of colors, you'd expect some old British lady to be drinking her hot milk in it every night! Instead, with this super-simple bed, the totally unfrilly bedding, and those austere-looking nightstands and lamps, you get something that works for both husband and wife.

HIS AND HERS

Although I wanted to balance out the feminine and masculine in the rest of the house, I took the wife's dressing room and the husband's study to the extreme edges of designing for the sexes. In her dressing area (a third bedroom that we converted into a huge, highly enviable closet), we decided to just go for it. This space feels like a room where a very stylish New York City fashionista might hang out with her friends or retreat to read by herself. Hello, did I actually install purple carpet? Yep. And then I upholstered the sofa in that amazing Diane von Furstenberg fabric with crazy pinks, purples, and yellows. It's so girly but also modern,

We converted an unused bedroom into a glamorous dressing room with a custom sofa covered in a Diane von Furstenberg fabric and a Minnie Mortimer photograph. Yes, this is sort of over the top, but it works, especially because it's a private room.

with those vibrant colors and that flower photography by my friend Minnie Mortimer. OK, I'd never advise people to pile on this much fabric and pattern—or even these colors—in a public room, but private spaces give you license to glam it up. Closets, offices, and personal bathrooms are great places to let your inner decorating diva really come through!

To keep the scorecard even, I also created a highly masculine study for the husband. It feels so *Rockford Files* in a way that I love. The wood paneling was original to the house, so I wasn't going to touch it. Then I got this great desk from the *Mad Men* era and added things like the California coastline painting. And voilà, here is this retro-Malibu study where you can almost *hear* the ice cubes dropping into the cut-crystal glass.

The office has a mid-century *Mad Men*–like desk with a Nathan Turner for Dutch Touch California oil painting behind it.

ENTERTAINING AT THE BEACH

Invites set the tone for the entire party, so give them their due! For my Mediterranean-style beach party, I decided to use this watercolor look to evoke the sea in an unexpected way. Then the colorful font keeps it fun and modern. I get all of my invites done at papermonkeypress.com.

There are very few people who don't like a beach party. I mean, seriously, what is not to love about spending a day in the sun with great food and great company? The beach is the ultimate gathering spot, and it's the perfect place to practice the kind of chic and easy entertaining that I love most. There's just no point in planning something fussy when you're dealing with warm weather, salt air, and the ocean. This is about keeping it simple, avoiding complicated menus that require long cooking times, and skipping the fussy table arrangements. Trust me, when you invite people to a beach party, they're not expecting something fancy. They want it casual. And this also holds true for people who are throwing a beach-themed party from an inland location: You want to evoke that laid-back vacation feel that you can only get by keeping it simple and stylish. Here are two beach parties I threw: one at the beach, one inland, and both with a totally coastal vibe.

ST. TROPEZ, MALIBU STYLE

I love the South of France, so for this party I took that theme one step further by looking to its famed Club 55 for inspiration. It's my favorite old-fashioned St. Tropez beach club, that kind of quintessential place where you sit at the table in your bathing suit, drink rosé wine, and eat grilled seafood. I wanted to create that kind of day—without killing myself.

The preparation for the party was pretty much limited to doing the shopping the day before at just one supermarket. (No annoying missions to specialty-foods places!) Then, the morning of, I set the table. Truth be told, that took some time. I really wanted the table to feel special, and to evoke that South of France vibe with lots of bright colors. I started with some blue batik fabric, and then I put some netting on it. I know that may sound corny, but when it comes to entertaining, sometimes you've just got to go for it and have some fun.

When it comes to planning a beach party, here's the best approach: You have to keep it super simple (and delicious). If not, you'll be jumping up and down all day, running back and forth to the kitchen, worrying if *this* is hot enough or if *that* is chilled enough. So forget multicourse when it comes to entertaining at the beach. This meal was simply grilled crab and lobster tails, a huge crudités platter, cheeses and breads, and bottles of rosé on ice. Everything went on the table at the same time. And all the food could be picked at and nibbled on all afternoon. This way guests are free to do what they like: They can eat, go for a swim, and then come back and continue the meal. And as host, this means that you grill the seafood, put everything on the table at once, and that's it. The rest of the day you can enjoy the beach and friends without worrying about being some perfect host.

TAKING COVER

A word about tablecloths: A lot of times if I'm doing a party with a theme or am looking for something really special, like some specific shade of hot pink or whatever, I'll just head to the fabric store. It's so much easier to get just what you want, not to mention much cheaper than buying a dedicated tablecloth. You can use that iron-on hem tape for a finished edge or, if you're like me, just leave the raw edge as it is. For this table, I also added netting on top of the tablecloth for an extra nautical touch. It was just a few yards that I had bought at a fabric shop and then stored away. I love the way it gives this table a hint of a nautical edge without going overboard.

TABLE-SETTING DETAIL

Don't wait to have a matching set to throw a party! If you have a grouping of plates that share some type of color story (here it's all about bright, cheerful colors), it will look great! Don't sweat it. The other benefit is that mismatched plates instantly lower the formal factor at any gathering. People will have fun faster, guaranteed.

RIGHT: Me and my girls Minnie Mortimer, Michelle Kalisz, Tessa Benson, and Stephanie Turner.

LEFT: For a casual beach party, I wanted to layer on the bright colors. I started with some batik fabric from the fabric store, layered it with some netting, and then added non-matching hand-painted plates and platters.

OPPOSITE: For Daisy and Nacho's bed, I used Sunbrella fabric, which is resistant to pretty much everything.

CRUDITÉS PLATTER A LA CLUB 55

Who isn't sick of doing the same old crudités platter? Here's a way to amp it up without a lot of effort. I think it's one of the easiest and best-looking appetizers on earth. You use whole vegetables—literally a head of cauliflower, a whole bunch of celery, cabbage—and you put it on ice in a cork bowl. Guests then break off what they want to eat, and the veggies stay cold all day. Talk about low maintenance. Then I whip up a batch of mustard dipping sauce to go with it.

MUSTARD DIPPING SAUCE

½ CUP OLIVE OIL

3 TABLESPOONS YELLOW MUSTARD

1 TEASPOON HONEY

JUICE OF ½ LEMON

SALT AND PEPPER

Combine in blender and serve.

A MORE TRADITIONAL BEACH PARTY

Beach-themed parties work with or without an actual beach! For this get-together, which happened to take place in Beverly Hills, the client wanted more of an island vibe for her garden party. To create this table, I actually used Ikea curtain panels for the tablecloth. They were insanely affordable, and I love how those colors—the ivory, blue, and chocolate brown—evoke a sense of a tropical island beach. And that was my starting point. From there, that notion of island beauty informed all of the decisions, from the wicker chairs to the scalloped shells on the plates to the piles of shells scattered all over. The point is: Don't let a little detail like not having a beach house stop you from throwing this kind of party! A seaside villa isn't needed!

This kind of table might look complicated and difficult to pull off, but it really isn't once you know the tricks. First of all, I used two matching urns to give height and symmetry to the table. Secondly, I stuck with one kind of item—shells—but just kept repeating and layering them. Yes, this is sort of a "more is more" look, which isn't usually what I do, but I just loved how the more shells I added the better it looked. And who doesn't want to feel like they're on a tropical island, even if it's in the middle of the city?

This is just a basic store-bought curtain panel, but here I used it as a stylish tablecloth. Palm fronds and shells are all that's needed to decorate the table in a loose and casual way.

ABOVE: I strung up super-cheap paper lanterns using twine. I love the fact that they're different shapes. It adds instant visual interest.

ABOVE: Sand-filled hurricanes and lanterns make the best nighttime lighting.

To get a party started, nothing is cozier (or simpler!) than sitting on the floor. Here, I created a cozy outdoor lounge with pillows, blankets, and rattan stools for side tables.

PART TWO

CITY LIVING:
Low-Stress Sophistication

FUNCTION OVER FORMALITY

MOVING TO LOS ANGELES TEN YEARS AGO OPENED MY EYES

to a whole new kind of city living. Unlike any other place I've experienced, L.A. really gives you permission to make your home however you want it to be. If you just drive down the streets here, you'll see mid-century houses beside Tudors and Spanish-style homes. But what became even more fascinating than what was going on outside these houses was what was happening *inside* them. After years of decorating in pretty much every architectural style out there, I came to realize that nobody needs to feel constrained by the architectural design of their home. But so many people do, which means their homes can become formal and rigid and, worst of all, fail to represent the people living in them. The key to the whole design thing is that there are no strict rules, even in cities like Boston or Chicago, where architectural pride is deeply a part of a city's identity. That is great. Embrace it if you're inspired to, but remember, this is your home, so I'd say the ultimate goal is to be super comfortable and stylish, and then maybe add a nod to the architectural style. Put it in that order. Don't put architecture first. You're the one who has to live there.

These days, rooms need to be extremely high on function and pretty low on formality. Let's be honest: We're all so busy, so what we want from our home is space to hang out, lounge, and relax. And I just don't see most people doing that on some overstuffed silk settee. No way. I'm more about taking formal living rooms and just saying to hell with it, let's put a big TV in there with comfy furniture and have another hangout room. The key is you've got to *use* rooms. So what will it take for you to use every square inch of your home? Be honest with yourself. If a flat screen is the answer, I say go for it. Or maybe you really love antiques. *Use* them. Don't hide them away behind some glass cabinet. If there's one consistent mistake I see people make, it's overdecorating spaces to the point where they feel like they can't use the darn rooms. I started out in antiques, and people are always surprised by how I use them. I manhandle them. That's why I like them. Chairs, tables, and accessories: I'm not afraid of really using them every day. Even if the worst-case scenarios happen—something rips or tears and punctures or stains—it's OK. You get it fixed.

But creating rooms that are highly useable doesn't mean sacrificing style. Just because you've got a family room where you're going to watch football games and have pizza night doesn't mean it's got to be dumpy. And here's an important lesson: It's your home. Enjoy it! It should be enjoyable. It's the place where you are going to spend a lot of time.

THE RULES:
GOING NATE-IVE IN THE CITY!

1. Space is often at a premium in city homes, so give rooms more than one function: Think of combining a library-dining room, kitchen-dining room, or bedroom-office.

2. Don't buy into formal spaces if you're never going to use them. If you're only going to use that formal living room two days a year, don't do it. I'd rather see a TV in a room with people watching it than some perfectly designed museum parlor that's always empty.

3. Respect the architecture; don't be a slave to it. So you live in a Georgian home. Do you have to re-create history? No way. Add your story and style to the space while acknowledging the architecture, and you'll get something that's truly yours.

4. Mix eras. Your house is not a movie set. If you live in a Spanish-style home, it doesn't need to be all about Spanish furniture. Mix it up. One or two on-the-nose era pieces per room go a long way. More than that, and your house starts to look like a period showroom.

5. Go for color: More than any other locale, city-living spaces need color. It's the fastest way to cheer up our hectic lives. Most of us who live in the city cherish every last minute we get to spend in our homes.

BRINGING A PLAIN BOX TO LIFE

ABOVE: The tablescape on top of the enormous upholstered ottoman in my living room is a constantly changing work in progress.

OPPOSITE: For this vignette, a mix of eras, styles, and materials is unified by a limited color palette, which keeps the look clean and interesting.

When I moved into my place in L.A., I immediately recognized that it was a box. OK, a 1960s mid-century modern box, but still, essentially, just a series of plain rooms without any architectural detailing or beautiful lead-paned windows. News flash: Most of us don't live in architecturally significant homes. But the truth is, I like the design challenge of plain-Jane spaces and think that with some clever, easily executable ideas, you can really transform a soulless space into something with energy, purpose, and personality.

One of the first things I did here was create faux-architectural interest with paint. This is one of the easiest and cheapest ways I know to give a room some instant personality. When I went to Istanbul, I noticed how in so many spaces they put tile halfway up the walls in the fancier rooms, and then in the more basic rooms, they'd simply re-create that effect with paint. So I did that here, going just three feet up from the floor with Benjamin Moore's "Coconut Skin" color. (You could really do just about any color to get this effect.) It's like instant wainscoting for a fraction of the cost. And best of all, it allows you to have two wall colors; one can even be dark, like this brown, but it doesn't give that oppressive feeling to a space. It just adds color and visual interest.

Another challenge in these super-basic rooms is to give them a sense of composition. It's not like there are built-in nooks and alcoves to work with. This is true for most of our homes, so the trick is to really let furniture placement do that kind of work for you—to create those little areas of coziness. Here, I opted for a pretty enormous sectional with an oversized ottoman coffee table to carve out a generous hangout space for lounging and entertaining. I love sectionals and use them a lot because they're so insanely comfortable, but here's the trick to making them *not* look like a *Roseanne* rerun: You've got to stick with a simple design. It's a lot of furniture and it's going to dominate the room. So keep it clean-lined, something that doesn't have too much design to it (I'm talking no curved arms and no big '80s lines). Keep it simple, and let the other furniture—the chairs and occasional tables and all that—be visually interesting. It helps offset the fact that you've got this massive sofa in the room. The other thing I like to do is to layer items like Turkish blankets and horse blankets over sectionals to help break up their massiveness.

In my living room, custom-painted lampshades tie in to the clean color scheme and echo the wall treatment.

Once I had the seating worked out, I could focus on bringing in some of my favorite things. Surprise, my favorite part! Bringing in the stuff! At first I really tried to keep the amount of things to a minimum. But little by little, I started layering in items: more books, more objects, more things on the wall. And I think that's actually important when you're dealing with these kinds of plain places that are so low on architectural detail—you have to bring in stuff! Now, if this were some fabulous Federalist cottage or a to-die-for prewar structure or something like that, I could see going the minimalist approach and letting the architecture be the star. But here, it was just white walls, basic windows, and no crown molding. So stuff became a way to bring the space to life.

CREATING AN ART WALL

Another huge decorating challenge for many people is how to approach that daunting bare wall. The key thing to remember is that there is no single right answer, and I think these two photos prove that. In one, I simply hung two large rose photographs by my friend Oberto Gili. They're super modern and simple. And they're also big enough to satisfy the scale of the room. Done, I thought. And I could have stopped there and had a perfectly beautiful wall statement. They adequately filled the space. People too often take a huge wall like that and hang two small pieces of art. The other most common mistake I see is that they hang pieces too high. The key is to hang items at eye level (and no, I'm not talking to professional basketball players). One night when I was home, I thought, "OK, I'm just going to hang these two little things up next to the rose photos." Cut to midnight, and I'm still hammering away, pretty much taking up every inch of wall space by hanging things as disparate as Mexican lotteria tins that I bought in Mexico City and a nineteenth-century terra-cotta Italian intaglio. The pieces don't necessarily "go together," but the mix works: small, big, colorful, black and white, angled, and circular. In creating these kinds of walls, start with your anchor piece(s) and slowly build outward. Better yet, lay the whole thing out on the floor, and it will give you a real sense of how it will fill up the space. Play around with it like a puzzle. So which is the right way to do the wall? Either, I say!

PAIRS, YES; SETS, NEVER!

Hate to be blunt, but sets are just never OK. I'm talking bedroom sets (matching bed, night-stand, dresser numbers), sofa and chair sets, dining sets—the works. Trust me, I'm not being a snob. It's just a bad idea and immediately gives a room that generic, chain-hotel vibe. But when it comes to buying a pair of things, I'm all for it. Symmetry is a decorator's favorite trick and can instantly give a shapeless room some sense of composition, whether we're talking two wingback chairs, a duo of urns, lamps, occasional tables, whatever. Designers always leap for the pairs. And rooms just need balance in general. But here's my trick to symmetry: I try to keep it relaxed, not too perfect. So I may put in a pair of identical chairs, like these in my living room, but then I'll do something small to make sure that they're not mirror images of each other, which immediately makes a space feel rigid. Here, I added a throw to one but not the other: something small, but just enough to make the moment feel imperfectly human and warm.

Then there's the issue of scale, which is an important one: The clutter mistake most people make with any kind of tablescape or picture hanging is that they don't vary the scale enough. If you're going to have a lot of objects on a surface, you need different sizes and styles so that it doesn't look like a clutter ball. Always have one or two big items, and then group little things around it. This makes a space visually appealing and creates some type of order that is calming, not chaotic. Like the antique English campaign chest in my living room. OK, there's barely room to set a glass on it, but I think it looks more interesting than cluttered. I started with a lamp for functional reasons, and that gave me my basis of height. From there, I added some smaller items but realized that the spaces were uneven with the lamp and the boxes, so I added the antique papier-mâché globe that gave me the perfect height and started creating that gradation of heights that makes little vignettes like this feel right. Keep in mind that you should always have more small objects than big ones.

A TRICK TO UNFUSSY WALLS

I bought this cool California flag at a junk shop. What's not to worship? I love this state, and the flag just has this amazingly cool, iconic look to it, so I wanted to hang it in my living room above the sectional. My original idea was to frame it in Lucite (read: not cheap). But in the meantime I just decided to tack it right up on the wall, unframed. And surprise, I loved the way it looked. Then I thought, "OK, I'll leave it up there but I'll anchor it with other stuff to make it seem groovy." Now I realize that framing it would have made the flag seem too precious. But I surrounded it with stuff that's more elegant looking; if I had started putting up posters, this would have been straight back to the dorm room. And I think this is an important trick to creating collections and grouping items: Put something super raw and unfinished next to stuff that is more polished, and you get this great-looking tension (and can save money and time to boot).

But of course there are some rules when it comes to filling in a space. Clutter is *not* the goal. Bringing in a warm and cozy feeling with lots of visual interest is. So how I did it here, and how I'd encourage others to do it in a similar kind of home, is to first create a sense of cohesiveness through color. That's how I start every project. Here, it's about brown, green, and white. I really stuck to that, and it helps give the room some sense, even with this much going on. OK, there's a pop of pink or purple here and there, but if you look closely, I stick to this palette. What's the right color scheme for you? This can be a scary question for many people who feel like they don't even know where to start when it comes to establishing a color palette. I always advise people to look in their closet to discover their comfort zone with color. I know mine—blue, tan, and white. It's what I wear all the time and—surprise!—those colors are often included in my interiors. If you feel good wearing certain colors, you'll feel good living in them. Pick two star colors (think of them as a leading man and a leading lady) and then cast a funny best-friend color (like a pop of orange) that won't get as much play but will still make an impact. Here, it was white and brown as the stars, then the pop of green in the supporting role.

No silver frames on the piano here! This is the only way I do family photos: in uniform frames on one wall. Here, I used the hallway in my house.

ABOVE: It's all about imperfect symmetry in my guest bedroom. The lamps, the artwork, and even those faux deer heads are all given details so that they don't mirror each other too perfectly. The non-matching bedding and headboard patterns also give the room an approachable sense of informal comfort.

One of my all-time favorite ways to ensure that clients are using every square inch of their homes is to give rooms two functions. That might mean putting the dining table in the kitchen, or putting an office in the family room—whatever. In the case of my dining room, it's got three functions. I had floor-to-ceiling bookshelves built in (not cheap, but I also could have installed a ready-built shelving system). It's all open shelving on top and then cabinets on the bottom, where I store my fax machine and printer. That lets me use the dining table as my desk. Then I can easily bring my laptop to the dining table or take it off and have dinner with friends. Library, office, dining room—love it.

THE DINING TABLE CHEAT

I see a lot of clients pulling their hair out over what kind of dining table to buy. And I get it: It can be a big investment. But here's an insane shortcut that I took at home that works so well. I just bought a sixty-inch round catering table. They're about one hundred dollars. No joke. Then I had a heavy canvas table skirt made and had a piece of glass cut to fit on top (that also limits the amount of times I have to clean the tablecloth, and it creates a better work surface). The total cost for everything was under $500, but here's the best part: There's storage under that tablecloth! I always end up putting work things, boxes, whatever, under the table, where it's completely hidden. Because the table isn't anything special, I elevated it by adding some nice antique chairs to the mix.

I admit, I took the master bedroom a little over the top. But I had to. Going to sleep in an underdecorated white box just isn't my idea of a good time. So I kind of went with it here. The main thing was to give some sense of architectural interest to a room that didn't have any of that going on. Hence the four-poster bed, a copy of an English Regency piece that I had in my shop. Then I added that curtain to the back of the bed by just Velcroing the material to the posts. It's white corduroy on the outside and on the inside a slate blue cotton that matches the wall color perfectly. I think it was that touch that finally brought some structure and shape to this shapeless room. Then I started adding my framed photographs. I kept going and going. I have a lot of them, but the other trick is that, since I'd painted the room a pretty dark color, adding those framed pieces effectively covered up some of the paint color and helped lighten the room. It's a great way to get both the richness of a deep color without a sense of doom and gloom. And note when I said "no sets," that extends to bedding. It just looks too fussy to have bedding be all matchy-matchy. So here I have this linen duvet that I paired with embroidered pillows. I love how it looks interesting, but not perfect.

OPPOSITE: Seating at the end of the bed creates a cozy en suite bedroom vibe. This is a Napoleon III sofa with a Carolina Irving pillow.

THIS PAGE: A bright orange phone from the 1970s is a great foil for all the antique Grand Tour photos.

MID-CENTURY MADE OVER!

ABOVE: Ione Skye at home with her dog Jack. Ione was a client whose inherent sense of casual sophistication worked as inspiration for the entire project.

OPPOSITE: The Danish bar in the living room is one of the few, on-the-nose mid-century pieces I put in the room It's all you need.

Ione Skye's home was the first mid-century house that I designed in L.A. And I'll admit it: I was scared. I'm such a lover of stuff, and most of those mid-century places in Los Angeles, with their stark lines and industrial materials, have like five things in them. But this ended up being such an important project for me in terms of opening my eyes to the fact that homes don't have to be enslaved by their architectural style to be functional and stylish. Let's be honest: Do you really want to live in a mid-century museum? Or a Colonial one or a contemporary one or *any* kind of museum? A lot of people would walk into this post and beam, with its great windows and open plan, and feel like they had to take the architecturally reverential route—especially here in L.A., the birthplace of this kind of design. And Ione had already done that, to a point. There were Noguchi tables and B&B Italia furniture. All gorgeous. But not necessarily perfect for a young, stylish mom with a musician husband, two kids, and two dogs who want to really use this house—as in run around, have friends over, play, and maybe even make a mess.

So I (gently) talked her off the architecturally reverential ledge and devised a plan that would bring in comfort, color, *and* function immediately. We decided to get rid of some of the priceless mid-century pieces and go for more durable, kid-friendly seating in equally strong fabrics and bold tones. Finally, I played around with the composition of the rooms to make sure that the family used every square inch of this house. Did I reference the fact that this was a mid-century house? Of course! I put in some classic, era-appropriate Danish modern pieces throughout, but very sparingly. And that's really all you need to give a nod to the home's design. A piece here, a piece there, and that's reference enough. Otherwise, I always look to the people who are *currently* living in the house, not to the architect who designed it half a century ago, to inform the majority of my decorating decisions. And I think that's the way all of us need to approach our living spaces: How do we want to use it? Not, what was the architect-builder thinking when he designed it?

OPPOSITE: Modulated greens and yellows keep the living room with its original fireplace fresh. The flokati rug is from the Rug Company, and the stone-top brass coffee table is from Lawson-Fenning.

THIS PAGE: In the master bedroom, I used Peter Dunham's Fig Leaf fabric to set the tone for the indoor-outdoor vibe that we created throughout the house. Claremont's graphic pillow brings a hit of pattern to an otherwise pared-down bed.

This house is essentially a glass box surrounded by a lot of lush greenery. I was struck by the fact that everywhere I looked, there was so much foliage: banana trees, bushes, so much. And I thought, "I don't want to fight that beauty with too much going on inside." So I decided to use greens and yellows in the living room. And I know that sounds like a potential disaster waiting to happen, but there are some really easy ways to use color without entering *Romper Room* terrain. The key is to vary the shades of the chosen colors. So in the living room, I didn't use just one green, I used three differing shades; and instead of one yellow, I put in two. And I did those different colors in different textures and fabrics. This is a different approach than the one that I took in my home, where I chose two stars and a supporting color. Here, I took one color, in this case green, and used it in three different ways. The effect? It gives a room a more modern look and keeps it interesting, not monochromatic. Using a bright tone on its own without gradating can make a space look like a preschool. Gradating color gives interest and depth. Put it all together, and it adds depth and punch to a space while preventing it from looking like a candy shop. But notice that I kept some of the big pieces, like the sofa, in the neutral zone.

High style meets durability in the family room. The cotton-covered sectional is perfect for plopping down, jumping around, or cozying up for a movie. Plush carpeting extends the idea that this room is about kicking back in comfort.

The family room really had to be that: a place where all of them could chill out, flop down on the sectional, and get cozy. And I think this is a great example of a sectional that's so not *frat house*. It's got very simple lines, but it's so deep, almost as deep as a twin bed. And I love that, because this type of seating practically forces people to relax—to tuck their feet in, kick back, and get ready to have fun. I don't know anyone who doesn't love those big, deep, comfortable kinds of sofas. And it's just heavy cotton fabric that I sprayed with Scotchgard to within an inch of its life. (When you use a piece like this, just accept the fact that the kids are going to jump all over it, and you'll save yourself and the kids years of therapy.) With all of these changes together, I think we really helped transform this home from something that was beautiful to look at into something that is both beautiful *and* highly functional. By simplifying the furnishings, adding in bright colors, and installing basics that can really withstand wear and tear, I feel that this home is a true testament to the fact that family homes can be super stylish and highly practical.

MODERN, NOT AUSTERE

A lot of people live in modern homes but don't necessarily feel like "modern" is their vibe. Here's how I approach that with clients: I use color to warm up the spaces but keep the furniture clean and simple. Trust me, the last thing a modern house needs is fancy French furniture. So keep the lines basic, but give the space warmth through color and texture. It's a total cure-all for those austerity-home blues!

THEN AND NOW

For the kids' room, nothing is more mid-century than this hanging chair. It's quintessential to the era, but the curtains behind it add so much color and cheer in a modern, graphic way that just feels so exuberant to me. And the tension between those two elements totally works because those are colors that are true to the house's architecture but updated in a modern way. In the living room, I just added that mid-century bar, and that was the only piece of furniture in the entire room that was straight-up mid-century. It takes so little to give that nod. For me, going whole-hog era-specific is one of the best ways to make a space feel cold and impersonal.

ABOVE: A subway scroll adds a hit of industrial chic to the dining room with its Saarinen table.

ABOVE: I prefer beds with simple lines to complicated, frilly ones. For this master bedroom, I went with a Modernica bed to keep it clean and streamlined.

OPPOSITE: Ione's collection of mid-century glass makes a colorful backdrop while we lounge together.

CASUAL GLAMOUR

Amanda Peet lives in one of those classic 1920s Spanish houses that are pretty common in certain parts of L.A. It has great-sized rooms and wonderful windows—a dream home to go in and decorate. But again, I didn't want to let the architecture dictate everything. The clients are young and they had a brand-new baby. A young family doesn't want to feel like a decorator is coming in to re-create their parents' house. They want to create their own lifestyle and make their own mark. Having a new baby, new parents worry about safety issues (sharp furniture edges, etc.) and durability of fabrics. This is obviously something I take into consideration, but I also urge my clients not to let the presence of children in their home dictate the way they live. I cringe when I walk into a living room and see Fisher-Price everywhere. There's a place for everything. When I first walked in, it was all wrought iron and big wooden beams—heaviness everywhere. That's the danger of these kinds of homes. But again, the idea here was to honor that architecture while lightening it up and looking to the client for the ultimate design inspiration.

And here the client was someone who was both incredibly glamorous and totally down-to-earth. So the design had to pull that off, too. This was really about "the mix." And I know, I know, that's an overused term at this point, but really getting that mix right is important, and it's easy to pull off if you keep a couple of rules in mind.

In the living room, I grouped very different styles of furniture: There's an English-upholstered sofa, the Pierre Cardin coffee table, those classic wingback chairs, and an ethnic carpet. Nothing is too industrial, nothing is too girly, but there is tension here, and I think that keeps the room lively.

So how to make the mix work? One of the most important ways is through color. Almost everything in the living room is neutral. That brings in some cohesiveness and lets you group unlikely pieces together. Then we decided to just go for it with that pink-and-red striped sofa. Yes, it's a bold move, but the idea was to add some serious punch to the room that wouldn't be too overwhelming. (Hint: When going for bold color, a stripe is much more soothing than a pattern.) So I let that sofa be the color star of the room. It is on the feminine side, but if you look around, everything else is kind of masculine and doesn't have nearly as much color. Making these kinds of design choices that keep both partners happy is the decorating high-wire act that I live almost every day. Of course, it varies from client to client, but the truth is, couples don't have to sacrifice their individual styles to create stunning common ground. Here, I took one large feminine statement—that pink sofa—and surrounded it with industrial furniture, muted colors, and the husband's mid-century Pierre Cardin coffee table. That strikes a balance that feels neither too masculine nor too feminine. But you could also pull off this balancing act by excluding any colors that are too traditionally masculine or feminine. That works as well. Strike blue and pink from your palette, focus on more gender-neutral tones (oranges, neutrals, greens), and then select pieces that might feel more "his" and "hers." The color will tie them together into a happy union.

THROW DOWN

Call me crazy, but I'm a huge fan of throwing something on the back of a sofa. And, no, it doesn't have to look schlubby. Here's the rule: The throw needs to have some visual interest to it. Plain black shawl? Forget it. But a vintage textile, some great patterned throw, something boldly patterned—those are the contenders. And I think that adding this to the back of seating is a great way to relax a room. It keeps it unprecious. It's a little bohemian, but in a fresh way. If I find a really pretty piece of fabric, this is often how I'll show it off.

THE MIX: DECONSTRUCTED

I know this might look like a simple room, but there's a lot going on in this breakfast area. There is a vintage industrial worktable with chairs, furnishings that are highly practical but can feel heavy depending on the setting. So I hung that kind of girly French chandelier above to lighten it up and then put that antique kilim rug on the floor. Face it: A lot of wear and tear goes on here, so I wanted to choose a floor covering that wasn't too heavy, that could take a high chair without getting stuck, and mostly, that could be cleaned easily.

For Amanda's family room, it's much more about lounging. This is a place to kick your feet up and a place for the kids to play. There are big, wide cushions, built-in seating, and then lots of vintage linens. And it's obviously got a Moroccan thing going on, which is perfect for the low seating and lounging that I wanted to achieve here. But as with all ethnic-inspired rooms, you run a fine line. I didn't want it to look like belly dancers were going to come into the room at any minute. My advice to people when they're designing with a really specific style in mind is to be *influenced* by it, not a *slave* to it. I wanted a Moroccan-influenced room, not a Moroccan restaurant. So I added ethnic touches, not ethnic everything—right down to the pillows, where some of the textiles are Moroccan, others are French, and others are American. The key is balance: Adding in a mix of other elements that don't fit in with the theme (but are still complementary) is imperative. So here I did totally Moroccan-themed low seating but then didn't upholster it all in Moroccan fabric. I chose to put a universal striped ticking on it. That helps it stay away from a themed vibe.

OPPOSITE: Farrow & Ball wallpaper
on the bedroom walls adds a sense of
visual interest without too much pattern.
A vintage mercury-glass light and a
nineteenth-century Swedish bench from
Lief work together with a vintage quilt to
create a space that is all about soothing
the senses.

ABOVE: I'm a big believer in mixing
different kinds of woods. Here, in
Amanda's formal dining room, I put
together nineteenth-century Swedish
chairs from Lief and a nineteenth-
century Belgian table.

PHOTO FINISHED

Family photo walls can look great—or totally cheesy. For me the key is to mix it up so you're including old pictures, new pictures, solo shots, group shots—even art and mementos can look great if properly framed. The key to Amanda's photo wall is the conscious mixing of wood, gilt, and white frames to reference the fact that the house also has a mix of elements. A tip to achieving this look is to lay the arrangement out on the floor and create your grouping first, or use craft-paper cutouts that emulate the size of your art and tape them on the wall first.

WOOD WORKED

In the dining room I mixed Swedish chairs with a Belgian table, a Chinese console, and a French mirror—a serious mix that travels all over the world! But I like this approach so much better than dining sets, and even wood that's all the same tone. It breaks things up, and overall it's light and inviting. The lesson: Don't be afraid to mix different kinds of woods. Even adding painted wood furniture to the mix works.

Everything had to be green and sustainable in this house, so I relied on reclaimed terra-cotta tiles for the floors and Cisco Brothers, an L.A. company known for sustainable furniture and lighting, for lots of the seating.

don't consider myself a "green decorator," but for this project, the house was a LEED-certified remodel of a 1920s Spanish, so everything—as in *every last thing*—had to pass certification. I learned a lot about the reuse of materials that are out there and discovered lots of new green products, which was great. But I couldn't sacrifice style, either, and the lesson here was that you really don't need to. The biggest way I'm green is by reusing. Every time you shop at a flea market or a vintage store, you're taking something off the market instead of creating something new. And you can be creative and have fun with those things. There is so much fun to be had with affordable flea market finds and a little bit of paint and fabric.

Adrian Grenier wanted the look of the house to be highly natural, so the focus became all about staying within a broad spectrum of earth-toned colors and materials but constantly shifting from within that range so that it doesn't fall flat on the eye. I know that beige can be the default color for many people who feel afraid to commit to color. And neutrals *can* work. You just have to remember to offer different values and shades of the color, and to introduce different textures and shapes—that will prevent you from getting stuck in those dreaded beige doldrums.

I also played a lot with the notion of hard and soft materials to keep it lively. In the living room, the sofa is done in a soft navy blue linen (my one color to counteract all the neutrals in the room). It anchors the space and, along with the rug, helps soften the old tile floors that we installed.

WALL POWER

These mirrors are all made from reclaimed wood, and, while they don't match in shape, they work as a grouping because they're all made from the same material and finish. I loved the way they filled this space and had interesting shapes. Huge, empty walls can be so daunting. Here, the lesson is that expensive art isn't the only solution for a stunning wall statement. Similarly, in the staircase, there was a huge expanse of wall space. Another option that doesn't break the bank is to select a grouping of like objects that are large. Here, that turned out to be vintage school maps. They're affordable and they add so much color to the room.

ABOVE: For the master bedroom, I used a Cisco Brothers' tufted bed in a heavy linen covered with a vintage serape blanket.

OPPOSITE: Vintage maps from Mexico City go all the way up the stairwell and add a shot of color to an otherwise somewhat-muted project. The suzani-cloth-covered bench provides some pattern.

ABOVE: Adrian in the living room, sitting on a tufted leather pouf from Cisco Brothers.

ENTERTAINING IN THE CITY

ike many of us, I spend most of my time in the city, and I find that I can drum up pretty much any excuse to throw a party. While entertaining at the beach or in the country is really about embracing the natural surroundings, when it comes to city entertaining, I try to focus on creating a fantasy-like experience for my guests. Yes, I'm very careful when it comes to creating themed rooms, but when it comes to themed parties, I say, "It's just one night, so let's knock it out of the park." There's nothing subtle about this kind of entertaining. I say the more themed the better. Whether I'm doing Moroccan or Mexican, Indian or English, I love to extend those concepts down to the smallest details. It's part of fully committing to the experience and creating an escape and experience for guests that they're not going to have anywhere else.

MOROCCAN TEA PARTY

Any place that will let you sit on the floor is my kind of place, hence my passion for Moroccan-inspired design, with its profusion of vibrant color. And (I'm not lying here) doing this kind of dinner party is actually pretty easy to pull off, even if it looks sort of fancy. Literally, all I did was cover my ottoman and set it as a low table and add a hanging light fixture. That was it for the décor. So little effort, but the impact is huge. And here's the other thing I love about a Moroccan party: People sit on the floor. Of all the entertaining tricks I know, this is one of the quickest ways I've seen to get people to unwind. You're taking your shoes off and sitting on a pillow. It's like skipping all the niceties and going straight to the fun, relaxed part of the night.

To make this table I just put a layer of cardboard over my upholstered ottoman to make a hard surface, and then I layered it with some ikat fabric. I then added an ikat runner in a different pattern. Again, this is just material from the fabric store. Cheap and easy. And I didn't even bother to finish the edges (although you easily could with hem tape). For the floor cushions, I bought a bunch of silk cushions from Chinatown in L.A. They were about twenty dollars each. Yes, I'm improvising here. Before you go out and buy things for a one-night event, give yourself time to really see what you have on hand. Sometimes things you don't think would fit into an ethnic theme actually do by way of color or texture. They might work even if it's not exactly on the nose. Here, for example, I wanted one more splash of color on the table, so I added some oranges off my tree with the leaves still on. It was that last bit of color that I wanted, and I didn't have to take a trip to the mall to spend more money. Not exactly Moroccan, I know, but the jewel tones work. And please, this is a dinner party. The idea is to have fun, not get caught up in literal details like the provenance

ABOVE: My huge living room ottoman turned into a dining table by my adding nothing more than a large piece of cardboard to provide a flat surface. Non-matching ikat fabrics create a layered, colorful look.

A vintage silver Turkish teapot with traditional Turkish tea glasses is set for service.

of floor pillows! I made a simple, prepared-ahead-of-time dinner of chicken tajine, couscous, and a big salad. For dessert I served an amazing apricot rice pudding compote.

And, yes, that *is* a Moroccan lantern hanging down over the table. I had it outside, but, deciding to go the extra mile, I put a hole in my ceiling and hung the light. A bit over the top? Maybe. But once I put a candle in there, and then put candles on the table, it immediately transformed the room into this magical space that makes everyone look beautiful. (And when I was done, I filled the hole with some Colgate toothpaste. Another decorator's trick!)

CENTERPIECE 2.0

In general, I love mixing things in with flowers for my centerpiece. For this Moroccan party, I immediately thought of fresh fruit and mint, so why shouldn't those elements come together to create an original (and totally affordable) centerpiece? It looks so lush, and it's incredibly cheap. Here I combined oranges, mint, and peonies, but you can really do this with any combination of fruit and herbs. Add flowers, or not. Another trick that I love is to take one of the centerpiece's elements and extend them down the table. Here, I did that with oranges, leaves intact.

MEXICAN TACO FEST

Another very low-effort, high-impact party is a Mexican fiesta. It's so easy to execute and is inexpensive across the board. It's all about having fun and enjoying delicious food and drink! I'm sorry, but I just don't know very many people who don't love tacos and margaritas. And building a taco buffet table means that, as a host, you won't be running around serving people. Everything is self-service. I even make huge pitchers of margaritas ahead of time so people can just help themselves.

Of course, the other reason I love to throw a casual Mexican fiesta is that it's one of the few times you can mix bold colors and get away with it. For this party, all I did was set up the buffet table (a long folding table covered in a bright piece of fabric), which I then anchored with two urns filled with huge kumquat branches. I love that pop of color. Then, of course, how could I resist hanging *papal picado*, those strings of brightly colored, cut tissue paper that cost next to nothing? Hang a couple of those, and they instantly transform a space into a party.

OPPOSITE: The indoors come out onto my patio with pillows and Mexican textiles. I used lots of bold color everywhere, and topped it off with *papel picado*, which hangs from the ceiling. It's cheap, super colorful, and fun.

BELOW: To completely set the party off, I hired a ten-piece mariachi band. Here's my cousin Stephanie with them. Live music is such a mood maker for entertaining. (Note: Mariachi music is loud! I insisted on long breaks so that people could actually chat in between.)

A CASE FOR CARNATIONS

OK, so carnations have a pretty bad rap, but done right they can look so fabulous. What I do is use one color per vase, then pack them in super tight. Here, I used pink and red carnations in a variety of vases. It ended up looking like a chic pop of color, and they're one of the cheapest flowers you can get—plus available at the supermarket!

NATHAN'S ROASTED CORN
GUACAMOLE

2 EARS OF CORN

4 AVOCADOS

½ WHITE ONION, CHOPPED

½ BUNCH CILANTRO, CHOPPED

1 SMALL JALAPEÑO, DICED

1 SMALL POBLANO, DICED

4 SHAKES OF TABASCO

JUICE OF ONE LIME

SALT AND PEPPER TO TASTE

Grill the corn on a BBQ or stick a fork in it and just put it over the gas flame on your stovetop. Cook until it's black and roasted. Let cool. Combine all other ingredients in a bowl. Just before guests arrive, cut the corn off the cob and stir in the kernels. Extra-credit ethnic points if you serve in a *molcajete*, one of those volcanic-rock mortars.

NON-CHEESY CRAFTS

Tiny details add up to make parties truly unforgettable. Here are two details that are simple, chic, and cheap. For this votive-candle piece, I bought the cheapest votives I could find and then went to The Paper Source and got a bunch of different colored and textured paper. Then it was just a matter of gluing the paper to the votives and stacking them on two wooden cake stands. Done. A big statement for very little money and effort. Then for the cutlery sets, I bought colorful, super-basic wrapping ribbon in all the colors I was using, and I bought corn husks at the market. I then wrapped them around each packet of cutlery and linen napkin. Again: on theme, quick, easy, and cheap.

For seating, I just dragged two twin mattresses from inside my house and covered them with fabric. So many people wait until they've got all the perfect patio furniture (which will probably be sets). I say don't let details like that hold the party back. Once I plopped a few pillows on these "sofas" and dragged an indoor coffee table between them, I had an instant area for lounging, eating, and drinking.

When I look at the photos from this magical night, it's hard to believe that my gatherings at the shop started with such humble, six-person-dinner-party beginnings. This was an official blowout, one that required tons of planning, lots of help, and, yes, some serious shortcuts that I think anyone could use. After traveling to India, I was so taken by the country, its people, its food, and its amazing use of color. I decided that I wanted to bring that back home, and what better setting than my shop, that ultimate canvas that had taken on so many entertaining identities over the years?

So I decided to do a huge party and invited about eighty people. I'm not going to lie: This took a solid month of planning. I ended up hiring an Indian wedding planner to help me with lots of the elements, and together we turned my store and courtyard into this Indian fantasy land that had just about everything but the elephant. (Not that I didn't want to have the elephant, mind you, it's just that I'm too much of one of those freaky animal-rights people to have some poor creature standing in as a party accessory.)

One of my primary inspirations was marigold flowers. I know, crazy, right? They're totally inexpensive, and they're everywhere in India, so I used them as design inspiration that I carried through the entire event, starting with the invitations. Keep in mind that for casual get-togethers, paper invites aren't mandatory. But when I'm doing something big like this, I like to set the tone right out of the gate, which for me means a beautifully designed, heavy-stock paper invite. It's the first glimpse of what lies in the future, and I like to give guests a taste of what's to come.

ABOVE: Always avoid fussy flowers. Here, I mixed blooms with mint to create a fragrant and laid-back centerpiece.

BELOW: Yes, I'm obsessed with the marigold curtain, a theme I extended all the way to my Indian party invite.

OPPOSITE: My beloved marigold garland and entry to the shop. I saw these kinds of garlands in India and ended up throwing a blowout bash just so I could use them!

One Kings Lane and Nathan Turner invite you to an

Indian Fête

to celebrate their passage to India
Saturday, October 2nd
7pm — 9pm

A buffet fit for a king. New and vintage copper serveware and a traditional Indian painting make it feel so authentic. (No one has to know that all of the food was takeout!)

COSTUME PARTY 101

I love a costume party, but not everyone does, and as a host your number-one rule is to make people feel comfortable, which means honoring all kinds of different comfort zones! For my Indian blow-out, I was hoping that people would be inspired to dress up, but I definitely didn't want anyone to feel pressured. So on the invite I added the line, "We invite you to wear your saris, cholis, or tunics." If you want to throw a costume event, it's a good way to do it; you're not forcing anyone to dress up in a certain way, but you're letting guests know that some people will, and you're giving them plenty of time to plan. That's how I like to approach it. I'm not into forcing anyone to do things, especially since everyone has a different comfort level, and this approach honors that.

This party had a lot of different areas and elements to it, so to keep it cohesive, I stuck to hot pink and orange. It's a very Indian palette, and all I had to do was buy yards and yards (and yards and yards) of inexpensive cotton in those colors. This is a great way to make a huge impact on a relatively small budget. Choose your colors, stick to affordable cotton, and use it to cover furniture, turn it into tablecloths, and even make DIY outdoor drapery. I rented a stunning tent by the L.A. company Raj Tents, but for the other two canopies, I just rigged them up myself using ten-foot-long curtain rods that I painted hot pink and tipped with gold. I sunk these into concrete-filled plastic tubs that had a PVC pipe down the center so that I could easily lower the rods into them. Then I swagged the fabric over the rods and added that fancy-looking trim I found at an Indian Market. I also used more fabric to cover the plastic tubs.

Obviously, when you're entertaining at this level, you have to budget in tables and chairs. This was a buffet-style dinner, but my biggest money-saving move for this party was that I ordered takeout. Takeout for eighty?! Trust me, a lot of restaurants will do this, and the amount of money you save by avoiding a caterer is huge. I've done this with Chinese dinner parties, Mexican parties, and pizza parties. It's one of my favorite tips. For this party, I ordered about ten dishes; luckily the restaurant was right near my shop, so they literally just walked it over. Presto, dinner for eighty was served.

OPPOSITE: Sad but true: I couldn't leave anything unswagged with marigolds—not even the adorable bartender!

ABOVE: The ultimate party favor—personal henna tats!

ABOVE: Refreshing ginger-infused cocktails garnished with mint.

The incredible Raj Tents in L.A. supplied the tents, lanterns, and furniture that turned my store's driveway into an unforgettable entrance.

PARTY: A SIT-DOWN TURKISH DINNER

After traveling in Turkey with my friend Soledad Twombly, I decided to do a sit-down dinner for thirty-six people in the shop. I hired a caterer to make the food so that I could focus most of my energies on creating a magical environment inside my store.

The big-impact move here was that I had a professional curtain person tent the inside of the room. Not cheap. But it wasn't a total budget buster either. Since I needed about one hundred yards of fabric for it, I used white gauze that I got for about two dollars per yard. Then that cluster of lanterns, which looks like it came from Aladdin's cave, is just a grouping of cheap paper lights that I got in Chinatown in L.A. I used all different jewel tones. The square silk pillows on the floor were also from Chinatown, for about twenty dollars each. And then I added Moroccan tea glasses and beautiful roses everywhere.

To create this low, twenty-five-foot-long table, I actually built it myself using four-by-fours as supports and plywood for the top. I drilled the legs in from the top and then used padding under the tablecloth to make a smoother surface. OK, so this was by no means legitimate furniture construction, but it not only lasted the night, I used it for subsequent parties as well. If you have the space to store something like this, building a long, low table is a great way to create instant atmosphere for all kinds of parties.

THIS PAGE: Garden roses from Rose Story Farm in Santa Barbara were used in abundance here. I mixed jewel tones and used tons of affordable, colorful glassware.

OPPOSITE: Simple cotton gauze was used to tent the entire back room of my shop. To add color and visual interest, simple Chinese lanterns were mixed with Turkish lanterns. Note those Chinese silk pillows—the same ones I used for my Moroccan tea party at home!

An Alessandro Twombly painting inspired
the table setting for this dinner party
honoring him and his wife, Soledad.

MADE IN WHEREVER

Yes, this was a "Turkish" party, but how many Turkish import stores do you know of? Even in L.A., I can tell you, there aren't many. So I decided not to worry about everything being perfectly Turkish and instead decided that I was just going to focus on jewel tones. This is key for great party design: Don't worry about every little detail; instead work toward creating spaces that have a big impact. It's those huge statements of color, or hundreds of candles or having people sit on the floor that will create the impression, not whether your salad knife is located in the right position or not. And besides, are your guests really going to say, "Why am I eating Turkish food while sitting on a Chinese pillow?" If they do, don't ask them back! Finally, the great thing about ethnic design like this is that most of the items are very affordable.

OPPOSITE: Quirky details make a big impact, so I decided to put a French fez on this nineteenth-century bust. And I know, fezes aren't exactly Turkish, but I couldn't resist this look.

ABOVE: I love entertaining with little plates. They not only look good, they also give people lots of options of new foods to try.

PART THREE

GOING COUNTRY:

Rustic California
Style Redefined

COUNTRY WITHOUT THE CLICHÉ

I COME FROM A LONG LINE OF CALIFORNIA CATTLE RANCHERS on my mom's side, which meant that during pretty much my entire childhood, if we weren't home, we were at my family's ranch in Northern California. Growing up there meant that I baled hay, roped calves, the works. Evenings were spent in the property's low and rambling home with wraparound porches and a vegetable garden off to the side. Meals mostly came from what was grown and raised on our land. This was farm-to-table living long before it was trendy. We also had a cabin in Lake Tahoe, where we would spend lots of time in the winter and summer. Both seasons are stunningly beautiful in Tahoe, an area nestled in the mountains and surrounded by lakes and pine trees. For me, it just captures that quintessential country experience and gave me a childhood full of winter skiing and summer hiking and fishing. And it gave me what is perhaps some of the greatest memories of all: coming inside after a long day in the mountains. There was always that fresh, woodsy smell inside—those good, warm interiors, hearty foods, and fires—all the essences of coziness. Even in the summer, at that high of an altitude, I remember not being able to wait to get into the cabin in the evening and sit in front of the fire. All of these experiences are what sparked my early love and affinity for the country.

When I moved to Southern California, I was no longer a quick car ride away from Tahoe and my family's ranch. Sure, I'd still go up for visits, but it became a once-in-a-while thing, not an every-weekend trip. That's how most of us live—*without* a view of lakes, wildlife, and mountaintops. But here's what I've learned: There's no reason why we can't bring some country into our homes no matter where we live. You don't have to relocate to a ranch in Montana to bring the outdoors in. Over the years, through working with clients in homes that are in the country and homes that are inspired by the country, I've come to realize that there are easy ways to make city spaces country cozy. Using some simple, easy-to-execute ideas, you can give any house an outdoorsy feel without it looking like a tragic Davy Crockett theme park.

THE RULES:
GOING NATE-IVE IN THE COUNTRY!

1. Remember that "country style" is hands down the most abused decorating style there is. I'm talking ducks on the doormat, too much plaid, and too literal a notion of what "country design" is. This is particularly important if you live in the city and are going for a country look. If you think country design can be bad in the country, it's double bad in the city.

2. It's vital to use less color and more texture in the country. And when you are choosing color, look outside for inspiration: We're talking tans, browns, greens, and blues. (And obviously I'm talking about the subtler versions of these colors, not the neon, pastel, or jewel-tone options!)

3. Steer clear of complicated patterns—certain plaids and stripes are the best kind of patterns. Nix the high-concept graphics and most florals.

4. Focus on bringing in a wide range of textures. I'm talking twill, wool, felt, heavy-woven linens, wood, leather—materials that have an under-polished, earthier, more organic, less-than-perfect feel.

5. Stay away from the idea that everything has to fit under the category of "country." I consistently use ethnic items, vintage pieces, antiques, sometimes even some extremely sophisticated stuff, and mix it all with other more straight-ahead "country" pieces. That's what can give your home a connection to the outdoors while at the same time provide a sense of depth, richness, and calm that's never theme-y. And "calm" is the key here. Many of my city homes have lots of bold colors and visual pop. They're meant to stimulate their inhabitants. With country, it's a different kind of vibe, one more geared toward contemplation, rejuvenation, and coziness.

NATHAN'S FAMILY'S HOUSE IN TAHOE

We don't have my childhood Lake Tahoe cabin anymore, but when my mom bought this place in Tahoe about ten years ago, it was a bit of a '70s wonderland—and not in a good way. But it also had classic high ceilings and good original wood paneling. Without insane amounts of effort, I was able to get it out of the disco era and into traditional country-décor turf. Of course, there were a few unexpected twists here and there. To get started, I established a color palette (here it was really about rich reds, tons of browns, some grays and tans). Then I began looking for a blend of country and ethnic items that captured all of these color requirements and gave the cabin a sense of personality. Case in point: Yes, I did put an antler chandelier in the dining room (don't worry, those are resin antlers). But that was it for dead-animal décor, faux or otherwise. There's no taxidermy, no bear rugs (not that I'd do that, either), just one classic country statement in the living-dining area. And that's my rule: Make one or two big "country" statements per room, then back off. Less really is more.

For the rest of the dining room, I used an antique farm table with English Windsor chairs at the ends and antique Swedish painted chairs elsewhere. I really love mixing up woods, but with country décor this is even more important. If you don't mix them up, these kinds of homes can turn into unidentifiable brown blobs with wood, wood, wood, everywhere you look. So vary not just the kinds of woods but the finishes, too (painted versus not painted, for example), to keep it lively and interesting. To finish off the dining area, I put in that rich red Turkish Tulu carpet. Middle Eastern accents in a country home? Yep. It works. The color is so rich (and won't show stains), and it's made out of goat hair. You can't get more natural than that! But mostly, the point here is *not* to sweat where things come from. So Turkish design isn't exactly a first cousin to English country décor. So what? It looks great, and I think it's exactly that mix of all sorts of pieces from far-flung places that come together to create a highly personal home. The point here is don't get caught up in being too literal. Establish your color palette and go for it.

OPPOSITE: My niece and nephews Lara, Henry, and Tommy in front of the river-rock fireplace at my family's Lake Tahoe cabin the night before Christmas. Don't tell the fire department—those are vintage Swedish Christmas candleholders on the tree.

ABOVE: Christmas dinner is served! Rack of lamb with roasted potatoes. Yes, I made it myself.

WOOD-PANELED WALLS

I've seen marriages practically fall apart over wood-paneled walls. It's typically the guy
who loves them and the wife who loathes them. But here's how I dealt with all that wood
at my mom's place: I left the paneling intact and unpainted (I mean, it does say "country"
unlike anything else), but I also decided to cover up a lot of it with art, rugs, and mirrors.
Why? To help lessen that oppressive feeling that this much wood can give. So up went a
Navajo rug on the wall in the living room; in the dining room, I mounted a huge mirror and
surrounded it with some traditional English country prints and paintings. Yes, it's all décor,
but it's doing double duty as a cover for some of that wood. It's the same with a bold wall
color choice: Go for it, but then cover some of it up with art and mirrors, and let those
objects mellow the impact.

In the living area, I kept the décor within a pretty traditional range. The sofa is a classically lined piece designed to get as many people lounging on it as possible. I covered it in basic brown corduroy, the essence of low-maintenance outdoorsy comfort, but I kept it from looking like a dated hunting lodge by adding plaid-upholstered armchairs. I then covered the side table with a suzani fabric. Again, the fabric is ethnic, not country, but the pattern is big and simple, and the colors fit in perfectly with my palette of browns, reds, and tans. That's the lesson: Connect your color palette with items that aren't necessarily country, and the elements will make sense and create a space that has visual interest. It also keeps it from seeming themed. Now, if I had covered this table in some crazy duck pattern, then we'd have been in trouble.

The ultimate kid- and pet-friendly living room includes a vintage Turkish Tulu carpet on the floor, a leather ottoman, and corduroy sofa. They look good, and they're built to last.

Lara and Henry relax on the bed in the master bedroom. The headboard is upholstered in a vintage Turkish wool textile, but I added modern, striped pillows to keep it lively, not dated.

In the master bedroom, I relied on the same kind of approach that I took in other parts of the house. I kept things rooted in traditional furniture with those English framed prints, the classical sconce lights, and a subdued palette of browns, tans, and beiges. But I added a couple of twists by taking a Turkish felt rug and using it to upholster the headboard. The rug is an old piece, but it's very graphic in a modern way, which lends itself to being mixed with these very modern red-and-white striped pillows. New and old, they complement each other because they both share that graphic line. Find the commonality between the new and the old, be it color, pattern, or material, and you can achieve a much richer, layered look that gives visual interest and personality. Again, there's not a lot of on-the-nose "country" décor here, but it works.

HOLIDAY TABLE SETTING

No, you don't have to pull out that Christmas-tree china to get some holiday cheer happening on your table. Here, I decided to do everything in red, but with different patterns. I used Ralph Lauren plaid plates that don't even match but work together because they share the red; people think you can't mix plaids, but it's surprisingly modern, and it works because they're all in the same color palette.

PLAID-I-TUDES

Some basic rules about plaid: I love it, and there's no better way to evoke that sense of fabulously casual country décor than with a classic check. But here's how I approach it: When upholstering big pieces in plaid (armchairs, sofas), I stay away from those really bright versions of plaid that can go garish so easily. I look for fabrics with less color contrast for the big statement pieces. Here, for my mom's upholstered armchairs, I actually used men's suiting fabric. It's got this faint patterning that just feels more subtle and soothing to me than some crazy gingham-looking print. From far away, you can barely tell it's actually plaid. I love that.

TOPIARY CENTERPIECES

Here's a super-simple, inexpensive centerpiece that lasts the entire holiday season. Get a simple Styrofoam ball from a craft store, then put a toothpick into a small crab apple and insert the other end of the toothpick into the Styrofoam. Repeat until the whole thing is covered. It's that easy! Here, I placed it in an antique urn, but you could fill up a basket or place a wooden dowel into it and put it in a pot like a true topiary. Be creative!

CLASSIC-STYLE COUNTRY
IN THE CITY

ABOVE: A Swedish painted console from Lief is adorned with Chinese pots, a French urn, and a grouping of antique oil paintings.

OPPOSITE: In this living room, "sophisticated" and "grownup" don't have to mean "boring." Gouache drawings by Vanessa Martin hang above a François and Company limestone fireplace. A pair of my cocktail tables, Nathan Turner for Elite Leather Timm's Cocktail Tables in slate, are functional and not at all fussy.

For this room, I was tasked with creating a country-style family room in a house that's located smack in the middle of L.A. The home is beautifully built, and best of all, it's surrounded by California oaks, visible from every window of this room. That obviously gave the room an instant connection to the outdoors, which I wanted to maintain through a decorating scheme that would be elegant, relaxed, and nature oriented. I didn't want anything to feel too precious or too colorful. The concept was more to create this space where you'd come in and want to read a book by the fire. And I get it: This is L.A. It doesn't snow here. You're not going to come in from shoveling the driveway in freezing temperatures and kick off your Wellingtons. But I think you can really get this country feel pretty much anywhere by using a mix of simple patterns, keeping a really earthy color palette, and layering it all with interesting antiques.

The overall key here is that nothing pops. There are no big colors, no crazy art; it's all subdued. But it's not boring. So how do you pull off a home that's soothing but not a snooze fest? It can feel like the million-dollar question for so many people who want something that is subtle and not trendy, for something that speaks to a certain elegance but isn't staid. I know it feels tricky, but here are the rules: The basic concept here is to offset a very limited color palette with lots of objects and a variety of textures. Otherwise you'll get one of those beige-on-beige hotel lobbies. Who wants that?

To get that layered, rich look, I displayed a lot. So when you're doing this kind of quiet, sophisticated country look, opt for open shelving and display pieces, not closed storage where everything is hidden. That doesn't mean you have to get some fancy bookcase or ornate built-in library. Here, I just put in a huge console and used that to display books. To me, this looks like an interesting person's English country house. And the nice thing about it is that all of those books are so easily accessible. The painting is by an American artist, Kevin Paulsen, whose work feels very American country, and that vibe anchored the tone of the room. But I'll be honest, I also chose the painting because the colors worked so perfectly with my plan. It's quiet and richly detailed—just how I wanted the room to feel overall.

A large-scale table from Lief with a
Kevin Paulsen painting above it makes
a massive statement.

PAINTED CEILING

This room had a domed ceiling, and I decided that I was going to paint it blue as a way of bringing in some color to the space without it dominating the entire room. And this blue is really complementary to these tan walls. (Besides, messing up paint is one of the cheapest decorating mistakes you can make. I say go for it with paint, and just do it all over if you've messed up. Better than getting wallpaper or upholstery wrong!) Painted ceilings are a great way to inject some color into monochromatic rooms without having that color take over. But here's the important lesson: If you're doing a contrasting color on the ceiling, don't paint the trim a third color (like white). Just extend the wall color to the trim and moldings so you've got a total of two paint colors, not three. I used the tan that was on the walls for the trim and moldings as well. If I'd done those in white, then your eye would have had three breaks instead of two. This is a more soothing, sophisticated approach.

I know a lot of people are afraid of decorating in a more monochromatic style. They're afraid it will end up boring and soulless. But notice that this room isn't spare. It's loaded with objects and different textures. There are things hanging on the back of the sofa, a mix of leather and linen and heavy tweed on the window seats. There are lots of subtle variations going on that are easy to miss at first glance, but spend some time here, and you'll feel the richness of it. Have faith in that; your room doesn't need to make a splash to provide years of comfort and coziness. You can have a quietly elegant home that is definitely not boring or stuffy.

Claremont fabrics and a vintage dhurri rug on the window seat add pattern and texture to a mostly muted room.

OPPOSITE: A small nook in the living room features a vintage suzani-cloth-covered settee. A floor lamp adds a nice reading-nook feel.

THIS PAGE: An eighteenth-century English chest of drawers from Lief paired with a vintage tea-tin lamp and antique framed intaglios from France give the room a layered, well-traveled look.

MODERN COUNTRY

ABOVE: A mid-century chaise lounge complements an antique pillar and antique pot.

OPPOSITE: Here, modern and antiques live together well because I kept the color palette limited to natural hues. I love this totally different take on country chic.

Here, I was looking to create a country-style home with a modern sensibility. I love that concept and feel that this is a great way for anyone to really get the best of both worlds: the clean, simple lines of modern design with the coziness of a country home, without an ounce of kitsch or overly traditional décor. There's no flannel or plaid here, no wood paneling, but it definitely says "country" in a different kind of design language. To me, this house proves that couples can have totally different styles and create a hybrid house that will appeal to everyone.

To lay the groundwork for this kind of melded design, start with bright white walls. That immediately establishes a canvas that says "not your grandparents' version of country." Then choose a mix of traditional and vintage design. What's great about so much mid-century furniture and accessories is that they're almost all done in natural woods or in an earthy color palette. In this room, there are no big color statements, but it feels incredibly fresh and modern because of the high contrast between those white walls and that clean-lined, modern furniture.

When selecting the furniture, I kept it to just browns and tans. That contrast with the white walls immediately feels more modern than, for example, my mom's Tahoe cabin, where the palette includes more colors that are all dominated by those wood-paneled walls. I also steered clear of a lot of pattern, another way to update country. And to keep this kind of "minimalist country" style from looking too cold or austere, I looked for slightly more worn vintage pieces; that patina brings in instant warmth and coziness. All of these vintage pieces have just enough age—the leather is cracked, the wood is notched—to feel that nothing just rolled off a showroom floor. These pieces have lived, and you can feel that. The sofa is new—just a traditional English-style piece with a skirt—but I added that vintage Turkish felt blanket to it for some texture and then used antique ticking pillows. The tree stump is from my family's original property in Tahoe, and it immediately gives a modern take on country décor.

NATURE-INSPIRED ART

So here's one of the best ways I know to get stunning art to your walls for almost no money. For these two contrasting deer profiles, all I did was buy a tracing projector from an art store (you can get them for under thirty dollars) and two plain canvases (less than twenty dollars each). I took a small image of a deer, projected it onto the wall, and painted onto the canvas with brown craft paint. Then I did the reverse. Done. Mega nature-art statement on a mini budget.

For the dining room of this modern country house, I used an antique Belgian dining table and an eighteenth-century Italian painted cupboard and mid-century dining chairs. Nothing matches, yet it all goes together.

One of the other huge advantages to this kind of modernized country décor is that you just don't need a lot of stuff to pull it off. Unlike other country projects, where I've basically loaded up rooms with containers full of things, this is both spare and cozy (and way more affordable to execute than more traditional forms of country design). In the dining room, I used little more than an antique Belgian table with Swedish mid-century dining chairs. And even if you're not using antiques, big-box stores carry all kinds of traditional- and mid-century-inspired pieces that would work just as well.

Here, there are no rugs, no window treatments, just simple anchor pieces that don't require a lot of accessories. That eighteenth-century cupboard adds some great texture and shows how, with antiques, the older you go, the more primitive the lines become, and the better they mix with modern things. I love that contrast. Even in the kitchen, we were able to be modern while keeping that warm, country feeling. By combining stainless-steel cabinetry with a butcher-block top, it's the best of both worlds.

PHOTO FINISH

A great way to give an outdoorsy home a modern twist is to feature photography that shows nature in extreme close-up. Here, photographer Oberto Gili's shot of a horse has a clean-lined, untraditional vibe because it's an extreme close-up in black-and-white. (Hint: 20x200.com has great black-and-white photography that doesn't cost a fortune!)

Antique ceramics and garden roses look rich against modern stainless-steel and butcher-block countertops.

ABOVE: Fresh nutmeg and meringue-topped eggnog get a style upgrade when served in a vintage silver punch bowl.

RIGHT: Canned spiced plums (yes, I canned them myself in Mason jars) with homemade labels (yes, to match the paintings)!

OPPOSITE: A modern take on a timeless French pastry: Here, I used store-bought meringues and applied them to a foil-wrapped cone using royal icing as the "glue."

HIGH COUNTRY CHIC
IN THE CITY

H ere was another "country" project located in the middle of L.A., where the goal was to create a room that would feel like its inhabitants had traveled all over the world. This is country design on a grander scale, and I'm not going to lie—it requires *a lot* of stuff: framed photos and artwork, furniture, rugs, lighting, accessories. Tons of stuff.

When I first walked into this room, I couldn't help but be impressed by its size and quality of craftsmanship. There are beautiful windows everywhere, and this room had those insane wood-paneled walls that I'd never mess with. So the question became: How could I really honor the architectural soul of the room without creating some total Jane Austen English manor? Again, how to get out of the theme-park trap? I decided to go for an exotic version of country that mixes many elements, including Indian, African, Middle Eastern, and American. Put that all together and it feels layered and original, collected over a lifetime, and not at all prescribed.

Can you mix all of that in one room without it looking like a crazy person lives there? Again, it all came down to color: Here, I really limited myself to essentially just browns and tans. That's how I was able to basically travel all over the globe in one room. The formula is this: The more influences you're going for (elements from different countries, eras, and styles) the more you need to narrow the colors and expand the textures. So since I selected from such a broad spectrum of styles, places, and textures, I was very strict with color and very open to all kinds of materials. That lets me have those African mud-cloth textiles on the throw pillows, and the Indian-inspired Ralph Lauren hand-blocked burlap wallpaper, and the Moroccan nail-head leather end tables, and that photography and artwork from all over. It works because the color palette is so incredibly narrow.

Another way to make sure that a quietly colored room like this stays lively and not bland is to keep things from getting too matchy. Those facing sofas, for example, are identical, but one is brown corduroy and the other is a heavy striped cloth. Because this is such a monochromatic color story, I thought that two brown sofas would have been so Debbie Downer. So my thought was, since they were exactly the same shape and style, I could have two different fabrics without it looking weird. It's a really good way to make a room feel layered and collected and look like it wasn't all done on the same weekend.

Even when it came to the window treatments, I went with fabric draperies for one set of windows and matchstick blinds for another. I do this all the time, and people are always surprised. Again, it's about layering and staying away from perfect symmetry. Here, the windows were differently shaped and required different treatments. Because the matchstick blinds are natural and read "quiet" in a visual way, they don't compete with the patterned drapery.

OPPOSITE: This huge-scale living room with high ceilings needed strong prints and well-planned furniture placement. I refused to use overscale furniture, which always feels impersonal. Here, Ralph Lauren's paisley wall covering helped deal with the enormous proportions of the room, adding a sense of coziness to its grandeur.

ABOVE: Vintage African textiles are amazing when used for pillows.

Once I had the furniture in place, it was time to bring in the stuff, lots of it. And I have to be honest with anyone who's wanting to do a look like this: You are going to need a lot of objects to achieve this heavily layered feel. I see so many people who lose steam when it comes to the homestretch of interior design. And I get it. They've spent a lot of money on the big-ticket items—construction, seating, lighting, storage—so they're not necessarily in the mood to spend even more money on all of the accessories that are involved in really finishing a room's look. But it's that last layer of design that identifies who the homeowners are, what their interests are, and where their tastes and style exist. So it's critical to budget in that last layer and not let it slip. Living in an almost-finished room is like existing in design purgatory—not pretty.

Here, there are at least twenty-five framed pieces of photography and art. That's a lot. I started with two large animal print photos. Those are huge photography moments that help anchor the identity of the room. Then I got one of those gallery screens that are available at Pottery Barn, and I loaded it up with a mix of oil paintings, watercolors, and photography, both black-and-white and color. They're all different shapes, heights, and styles. The way they lean, instead of lying flat, gives off a vibe that they've been casually collected over the years, not carefully positioned during an intense workweek! I love gallery screens and feel that they are an amazing option for people who want this layered look without committing to a photo-gallery wall. They really work, and they give you the ability to constantly switch things around without putting nails in the wall.

THIS PAGE: An Amber Arbucci photo paired with a globe and a mix of other objects creates that well-traveled-over-the-years look I wanted to achieve.

OPPOSITE: A custom-made screen is a great way to display art, photos, and other family treasures.

PLANT COLONY

I get it: Some decorators are adamantly against indoor plants. I'm not one of those people.
I think plants can give feeling to a room, and trees can create the height that you just can't
get with furniture. Here I put in a fourteen-foot tree and two huge ferns, which diffuse
some of the light coming in through the windows. Plant life also offers a nice respite from
all of the browns and tans here. And for anyone who's ever even contemplated buying
those horrible sticks that designers put in vases to give height to a space, I'm begging you:
Go for a tree instead! So much more stylish!

CUTTING THE BLUE TAPE

When you're approaching big rooms like this, blue tape is your best friend. I use it to work out where I'm going to put my furniture to make sure its placement won't hamper easy movement throughout the room. In rooms that are this big, your seating can get lost, so I use the tape to figure out where I'm going to create that focal seating point without using overscaled furniture. For me, those fourteen-foot sofas and Alice in Wonderland–size armchairs are just a huge no-no. They can instantly turn rooms into corny-looking nightclubs. Yuck. So I stuck with eight-foot-long sofas and normal-size chairs. The upholstered ottoman is large, but not to the point where it throws the seating out of proportion. Here I measured out two identical sofas, a pair of armchairs at one end, then one chair on the opposite side of the ottoman so that there's an opening point to the seating area. You don't want your seating to form an enclosed rectangle or square where guests are trapped! Seating should be placed to create a U-shape so that people can move around easily.

THIS PAGE: Another photo by Amber Arbucci hangs above a Portuguese console in the same huge-scale living room. My Nathan Turner for Elite Leather Candemir Ottoman is covered in Ralph Lauren's Serengeti Zebra fabric.

OPPOSITE: Here I am mixing drinks in the room's Prohibition-era bar. The bar stools are by Pottery Barn.

ENTERTAINING IN THE COUNTRY

Country entertaining is all about creating cozy environments and hearty comfort food. People tend to think that country entertaining is only about colder weather and warm fires (which it can be), but I think it's great all year. This is about rustic and casual gatherings that celebrate the outdoors and make nature the star of your décor, whether you're dining inside or out. It's the ultimate no-fuss kind of entertaining where you just go outside and bring the environment to the table. It's about going to the garden and putting herbs in mismatched vases or simply scattering apples around the tablescape. Country entertaining requires so little effort to create so much beauty.

OPPOSITE: My brother Matthew and sister-in-law Jolene with Dallas and Keto at my parents' Nevada home

BELOW: Just-picked apples and pears from my parents' place in Nevada.

Here I am in Nevada with my mother, my sister-in-law Jolene, my brother Matthew, my great-grandmother Marion—she was ninety-nine years old when this picture was taken—and of course, Daisy!

APPLE HARVEST DINNER PARTY

In September, we pull down all the apples at my mom's place in Nevada, and then we spend the weekend making apple butter, apple pie filling, apple chutney—anything to do with apples. I'll inevitably end up organizing a casual dinner to celebrate the harvest during the weekend. And for me, it's the essence of low-key entertaining. When I'm doing the table, nothing matches. Really, nothing. Not the plates, not the pillow cushions, not the glasses or the silverware or the chairs. I just put it all together based on what's available, and it ends up feeling like a great old-fashioned American table. This is all about really embracing the non-set. I don't even mess with flowers, place cards, or any of that for this kind of table. Instead, I just take some apples from the trees and play around with them. Then I'll grab some herbs from the garden, just little sprays of them, and put them in different types of vessels: a vintage milk glass or a granite cup that was used for gold mining. The great thing about doing this kind of dinner is that this stuff is all available at thrift stores everywhere. I'm talking Salvation Army here. When you take the "matching set" pressure off yourself, you can really go into any thrift store and create a stunning table for six or eight people for under thirty dollars. Trust me, the mismatched charm of it all will create dinner party magic.

My harvest dinner menu is as simple and effortless as the table décor. It's just Roasted Game Hens with Apples and Sage that I do in a Dutch oven (translation: Put it all together, and you're done), roasted potatoes, and a green salad. That's it. It all goes on the table at the same time so I get to enjoy the meal as much as the guests. Nothing more is required. For dessert, I serve both apple pie and my family's Spiced Apple Cake with Cream Cheese Frosting. We've been making it for generations, and what I love about it is that it requires no precision. The messier and more homemade it looks, the better.

LEFT: My cousin Jamie lounges with colorful vintage pillows on a Mexican serape blanket.

RIGHT My roasted chicken with braised apples and sage from the garden.

OPPOSITE: My brother Matthew with Keto the horse. I call my brother "the Horse Whisperer."

MARION'S APPLE SPICE CAKE

1 CUP SUGAR

1 CUP APPLESAUCE

1 EGG

1 CUP RAISINS

1 TEASPOON CINNAMON

1 TEASPOON NUTMEG

1 TEASPOON BAKING SODA

2 CUPS FLOUR

1 CUP CHOPPED NUTS

Heat oven to 375 degrees. Mix all wet ingredients. Sift in dry ingredients and pour into a greased pan. Bake for 45 minutes.

CANNED APPLE PIE FILLING

4 CUPS SUGAR

¾ CUP CORNSTARCH

2 TEASPOONS GROUND CINNAMON

½ TEASPOON GROUND NUTMEG

2 TEASPOONS SALT

10 CUPS WATER

JUICE OF 2 LEMONS

6 POUNDS APPLES

1. In a large pan, mix the sugar, cornstarch, cinnamon, and nutmeg.
Add the salt and water and mix well. Bring to a boil and cook until thick and bubbly.
Remove from heat and add lemon juice.

2. Sterilize canning jars, lids, and rings by boiling them in a large pot of water.

3. Peel, core, and slice the apples. Pack the sliced apples into hot canning jars,
leaving a ½ inch of headspace.

4. Fill the canning jars with hot syrup and gently remove air bubbles with a knife.

5. Put lids on the jars and process in a water-bath canner for 20 minutes.

OPPOSITE: Pears from the property, peeled and ready to be canned.

ABOVE: A mix of vintage cutlery and linens keeps the table simple but interesting.

ABOVE: My mother, Judy, with her famous apple pie.

ARGENTINE GRILL DINNER

I used Argentinian horse blankets that I found in Buenos Aires in lieu of place mats, and wooden cutting boards instead of plates. They instantly put guests in Argentinian grill mode!

Who can resist a great BBQ? I love throwing a low-key burger-and-hot-dog get-together, but I've also spent a lot of time in Argentina, where they approach the whole concept a little differently. And it turns out it's a super-simple and insanely delicious way to kick your everyday BBQ up a notch—without tons of effort. The Argentine grill is all about gaucho culture, which has similarities to the American cowboy scene, so I sort of borrow from both when setting the table.

Instead of tablecloths, I use horse blankets, and then I sub in individual cutting boards for charger plates. Those two elements are really all that's required to make a big and unexpected design statement without a lot of work.

You can use your existing grill for this meal, or you can build your own fire pit like I did. All that it involved was making a circle with stacked bricks and then setting a grill on top of it. Simple. Then I used a mix of mesquite wood and charcoal and was ready to get going.

The Argentine grill is really about mixing up different kinds of meats: Have a selection of skirt steaks, rib eyes, and fillets. That's how they do it there. Then make your own Chimichurri Sauce (recipe below) and have that on the table as the classic Argentine condiment. Make a corn soufflé ahead of time (classic South American side), and a huge green salad, and that's it. Everything is served family style so there's no running around. For drinks, I offered Argentine beer and Clerico, a white-wine sangria that people love.

CHIMICHURRI

1 BUNCH PARSLEY, COARSELY CHOPPED

8 CLOVES GARLIC, MINCED

¾ CUP OLIVE OIL

¼ CUP SHERRY WINE VINEGAR

3 TABLESPOONS LEMON JUICE

1 TEASPOON SEA SALT

½ TEASPOON FRESHLY GROUND BLACK PEPPER

½ TEASPOON CAYENNE

Combine all ingredients in a bowl and serve (can be made the day before).

I usually entertain family style, but here I made an exception (mostly because this salad bowl is so darned huge) and served my guests directly.

CLERICO

2 (750 ML) BOTTLES INEXPENSIVE WHITE WINE (NOT TOO SWEET)

2 BANANAS, PEELED, SLICED INTO 2-INCH SLICES

1 ORANGE, RIND RESERVED, CUT INTO SEGMENTS

6 PEACHES, PEELED, SLICED INTO 6 WEDGES EACH

1 RED APPLE, CENTER REMOVED, CHOPPED MEDIUM DICE

6 PLUMS, SLICED INTO 6 WEDGES EACH

2 LEMONS, RESERVE RIND, JUICED

1 CUP RED GRAPES

2 CUPS ICE

SUGAR

8 OUNCES SELTZER OR LEMON-LIME SODA (OPTIONAL)

Place all fruit in a large glass pitcher. Add 2 cups ice, lemon juice, orange and lemon rind, and white wine, and refrigerate until just before serving. At the last minute, add sugar to taste, and soda if desired.

OPPOSITE: One of my favorite DIY dining tricks in the world is making my own grill out of bricks and my grill top. It's portable and chic.

ABOVE: I love a self-service bar for almost every kind of party, as it keeps things casual. Here, I used buckets for Argentinian beer on ice and clerico.

RIGHT: Since this party was all about giving your basic hot dog cookout a stylish upgrade, I displayed the sausages on a carved wooden plate.

TORTA DE CHOCLO (CORN PUDDING)

2 EARS FRESH CORN

2 CUPS MILK

½ CUP HEAVY CREAM

2 TABLESPOONS UNSALTED BUTTER

¾ CUP YELLOW CORNMEAL

3 TABLESPOONS CHOPPED FRESH CHIVES

1 MEDIUM POBLANO, SEEDS REMOVED, FINELY CHOPPED

KOSHER SALT AND FRESHLY GROUND BLACK PEPPER TO TASTE

3 EGGS, SEPARATED

Preheat oven to 350 degrees. Remove husks from corn and put in a large pot with milk and cream. Set over low heat and bring to a simmer, then shut off heat and cover to let corn steep, about 10–15 minutes. Remove corn from milk and cut kernels off the cob with a sharp knife. Set aside.

Strain the milk mixture and set back over high heat; add butter and pour in the corn-meal in a slow and steady stream, whisking at the same time. Cook and whisk constantly until the cornmeal is blended in and the mixture is smooth and thick. It should look like porridge. Take the pot off the stove and fold in the corn, chives, chopped poblano, and salt and pepper. Mix in the egg yolks, one at a time, to make it more like a batter. In a separate bowl, beat the egg whites (use a hand blender if you have one) until they hold stiff peaks. Fold the whites into the corn pudding to lighten it. Coat the bottom and sides of an 8-inch baking dish with nonstick spray. Spoon the batter into the prepared baking dish and bake for 25–30 minutes. When it's done, the corn pudding will look puffed and golden brown, like a soufflé.

CHIC PIZZA PARTY FOR KIDS

When I was helping a friend throw a pizza party for a large group of kids, the idea was to give the get-together an old-fashioned country feel. OK, so the hostess lives in one of the most fabulous houses in L.A., but it's very contemporary, and with just a few targeted moves, we were able to give the backyard a relaxed, farm feel.

THIS PAGE: It looked as if I had been making pizzas all day, but they were actually generously provided by Nancy Silverton of Mozza2Go for our charity event benefiting the Garden School Foundation.

OPPOSITE: Me with my fellow hostesses Amber Valletta and fashion designer Jenni Kayne.

TABLE SETTING

All I did was cover the rented tables in burlap (totally inexpensive) and then put a Pottery Barn vintage grain sack down the middle as a runner. For the centerpieces, I used Pottery Barn's galvanized stacking containers and just filled them with fruits and veggies—the cheapest thing in the world—and the centerpieces also make great party favors. We used old camping plates to keep the feel rustic and relaxed.

So here's the trick: with this party, I wanted to have a really homespun and back-to-the-earth feeling. But am I really going to make pizza for twenty hungry kids? Heck no. So I took a serious shortcut that I've ended up doing so many times since. I simply ordered about two dozen individual-sized pizzas and made sure that they *weren't* sliced. Then I bought a huge slab of butcher block from Home Depot (also very cheap) and had it put on top of an existing table. When the pizzas arrived, I got rid of the boxes as soon as possible and laid the pizzas right on top of the butcher block for a slice-and-serve-yourself buffet table. No one needed to know that there were twenty-four boxes in the kitchen! And if you don't want to deal with butcher block, just lay out a roll of butcher paper on a table for a great way to display delivered pizzas as if you'd made them yourself!

ABOVE: Keeping with the garden theme, fresh berries make the ultimate fresh and healthy dessert for kids. These are from my favorite source, Melissa's (www.melissas.com).

ABOVE: Pottery Barn's galvanized pails instantly organize and chic-ify something as simple as bamboo plates and cutlery.

OPPOSITE: The galvanized plates have that quintessential throwback American look that I love. I always link my invitation to the party in terms of look and feel. And I always rely on Paper Monkey Press (www.papermonkeypress. com) for amazing invites.

CRAFT WORK

When I'm entertaining for kids, I usually steer clear of bouncy houses and hired entertainers. Let kids entertain themselves. That's how I grew up. So here I just went to Michael's and stocked up on pompoms, pens, pipe cleaners, paper, glue, and whatever I could get my hands on. I didn't even have a specific craft in mind. The goal was just to let the kids do their thing. Which they did, for a long time, while their mommies got a chance to eat, mingle, and enjoy themselves.

PARTY: A BLOOMSBURY PARTY, ENGLISH COUNTRY FALL DINNER

I'm seriously in love with the whole Bloomsbury aesthetic, and since I wanted to do an evening get-together to celebrate autumn, what better inspiration than the British, who I think have a monopoly on all things cozy? But when you zero in on the Bloomsbury look, I think it really makes for easy entertaining. This style is all about not worrying if things match or not, and combining great textures and lots of earthy colors. I feel that most of us have many of the elements needed for this kind of entertaining already on hand at home. It's just a matter of putting it all together. And if not, this really is stuff that can be found in a thrift store. The possibilities open up without the pressure of needing a complete set.

THIS PAGE: I love the wild look of these flowers in an antique iron urn. For me, they're the ultimate in Bloomsbury chic.

TABLE SETTING

For this party, I wanted to celebrate autumn with a cozy get-together. I had slipcovers made for the chairs in a floral linen and then used that same fabric for the tablecloth (totally unnecessary, but I couldn't resist). But that was it for anything that matched. After that, I assembled an array of plates and glasses as well as a mix of Splatterware jugs in all different colors—they're totally affordable and are such an effective way to bring a country vibe to the table. For the silverware, I used Pottery Barn's Maxfield Cutlery, which I love because it's actually a mismatched set that looks antique and collected over time. Love that.

I kept the menu really English and cozy. It was kidney pie, butternut squash soup in acorn-squash bowls, and for dessert, ginger charlottes and brown-sugar shortbread. That was it, along with red wine. I didn't put the pressure on myself to serve cocktails and wine. Casual dinners just don't require jumping through those kinds of hoops, so why kill yourself? And come on, you don't get kidney pie at every dinner party, but it's a cinch to make. It's those unexpected touches that can really help guests feel transported to another place by a party.

BUTTERNUT SQUASH SOUP

5 TABLESPOONS OLIVE OIL

2½ POUNDS BUTTERNUT SQUASH, SQUARED, PEELED, SEEDED, AND CUT INTO ½-INCH PIECES (ABOUT 6 CUPS)

2 CUPS CHOPPED LEEKS (WHITE AND PALE GREEN PARTS ONLY)

½ CUP PEELED AND CHOPPED CARROT

½ CUP CHOPPED CELERY

1 SMALL GRANNY SMITH APPLE, PEELED, CORED, AND CHOPPED

1½ TEASPOONS DRIED THYME

½ TEASPOON CRUMBLED/DRIED SAGE LEAVES

6 CUPS CHICKEN STOCK

2/3 CUP SOUR CREAM

Heat the oil in a heavy, large saucepan over medium-high heat. Add the squash, leeks, carrot, and celery; sauté until slightly softened, about 15 minutes. Mix in the apple, thyme, and sage. Add the stock and bring to a boil. Reduce heat to medium-low. Cover and simmer until the squash is tender, stirring occasionally, about 30 minutes. Cool slightly and puree in blender before serving.

OPPOSITE: English kidney pie isn't your typical dinner-party fare. Guests will be surprised, and no other easy, do-ahead dish makes for a cozier meal!

ABOVE: Old and new come together to create a great look. Don't be afraid to use brand-new items with very old. Here, Pottery Barn's pheasant plates mix with a nineteenth-century English china platter. Don't they look like old friends?

ABOVE: Braised kale with garlic chips and fresh cranberries is an easy-peasy side dish that is such a welcome change from the expected.

I wanted to host a little outdoor cocktail party along with Molly Sims for the British handbag designer Anya Hindmarch. I love her designs and, of course, the idea of throwing an English-inspired gathering was enticing enough in and of itself. We'd originally planned to throw it in the summer, but then schedules changed and it got bumped to February. Regardless, I was still determined to hold it outdoors. So it morphed into an outdoor, English-inspired winter garden party. I know, I know, very specific! But even though it may sound a little harebrained, I have learned that the more specific you go with your party inspiration, the more guests will have a magical experience. Yes, entertaining on this level is more challenging: I would never say that this party was a breeze or that I did it all myself on a shoestring budget. Not the case! But I loved the challenge and was determined to keep it elegant and original without completely killing myself.

More than anything, I wanted to create a large outdoor room in the shop's courtyard that would make guests feel as if they had stumbled into the garden of an English country home. I wanted it to feel relaxed and cozy, and the kind of place where you could gather around the fire and settle down for a good chat with friends. So out came a combination of outdoor and indoor furniture from my store. I dragged it all out, and then, to give uniformity to the mismatched pieces, I added faux-fur throws onto the seating. That instantly gave the "room" a sense of coziness. And if you didn't want to go the faux-fur route, you could always buy inexpensive cotton and simply tuck it under cushions to give mismatched furniture a more uniform look. Then I heightened that sense of an indoor room under the sky by adding table lamps and throw pillows to the mix. It's one of my favorite tricks for a cozy outdoor room: Use really nice indoor items outside. It's only for one night, so go for it! To top it all off, I strung those super-basic party lights all around. They're Pottery Barn's Café String Lights with this little galvanized canopy, and they're the ultimate way to make a nighttime party sparkle.

ABOVE: It's all about the details: I took Anya Hindmarch's logo and used it on the cigar wraps—a crazy-specific little thing to worry about, but all of the effort paid off.

BELOW: Me with Anya Hindmarch and Molly Sims.

OPPOSITE: Faux-fur throws by Pottery Barn literally covered every inch of seating to create this ultimate outdoor-lounge vibe. I wanted to make sure no one left early on a cold winter night.

So yes, setting up that outdoor space did involve some time and money. I also needed help to set it all up. (For this kind of room, you'd be crazy to think you can do it on your own. Whether you're hiring someone or are relying on friends, having help is one of the key ways to avoid a pre-party meltdown as a host.) To offset all of that effort, I kept the menu super simple. This was just cocktails in the English "country," so I didn't need to come up with a multicourse meal. I simply served mini shepherd's pies made in cupcake tins and nuts roasted over the fire pits in cast-iron pans. As a final touch, I made a s'mores bar, which people freaked over. I loved the idea of glamming up the camping staple by creating this bar with antique silver service and candles and antique accessories, but all of the ingredients just came from one quick trip to the supermarket (OK, those square marshmallows did come from a specialty store!).

Who says you can't glamp at your own party? I used a cast-iron skillet to roast nuts over an open flame. Guests could then just scoop up as much as they wanted in small paper bags.

SPICED NUTS

Serve-yourself bars are so great when doing low-effort, high-style entertaining. First of all, people love to build their own whatever (burger, hot fudge sundae, etc.), and second, as a host, you just set it up, and then you're done. People take care of themselves. But when you're planning a bar, you have to go for it. Just go a little crazy, and then people really get inspired. So for the s'mores bar, I had the basic marshmallows, graham crackers, and chocolate, but then I added caramel sauce, nuts, peanut butter cups, and marshmallow fluff. It was the hit of the party and created something of a frenzy!

SPICED NUTS

1 LARGE EGG WHITE

1 TEASPOON WATER

4 CUPS MIXED SALTED ROASTED NUTS (ABOUT 1¼ POUND)

½ CUP SUGAR

1½ TABLESPOONS CINNAMON OR PUMPKIN PIE SPICE

Preheat oven to 250 degrees. Whisk together egg white and water in a large bowl until frothy and stir in nuts. Stir together sugar and cinnamon and stir into nuts, coating well. Spread nuts in a lightly buttered, large, shallow pan and bake in the middle of the oven until dry, about 50 minutes. Cool and break into bite-size chunks.

ABOVE: Co-host Molly Sims admires the posies in horn cups.

OPPOSITE: My over-the-top, decadent take on s'mores. Here, I took a basic recipe and ran with it, even using my fancy English silver to display everything. Who could resist?

ABOVE: Forget fancy florals: Here, I took simple wildflowers, wove them into small wreaths, and put them everywhere.

ACKNOWLEDGMENTS AND CREDITS

Thanks to my team at Abrams: Rebecca Kaplan, my editor, for understanding me from the beginning (not an easy feat) and for letting me be creative, while keeping me organized (an even more difficult feat); Jennifer Brunn; and Samantha Weiner.

Thanks to Alexandria Abramian-Mott for helping put my jumbled California-speak down on paper, and for starting this whole mess ten years ago by writing the very first piece on me and the shop.

Thanks to my ICM team: Lori York, for always believing in my talents; Andrea Barzvi, for helping me navigate the world of publishing; and Carol Goll.

A huge thank-you to some of my clients and collaborators: Hilary Lindahl and Chris DeWolfe; Amanda Peet and David Benioff; Adrian Grenier; Collin and Claire de Rham; Ione Skye and Ben Lee; Julie Jaffe; Jennifer Lechter; Erlin Katuari and Ben Jiaravon; Christine and Bruce Greene; Diantha Lebenzon; Nancy and George Moss; Steve Loguidice and Robert Luketic; Melissa's Produce ("Auntie" Sharon and Joe); Susan Feldman; Allison Pincus; Andrea Stanford; Elite Leather and the Gallardo Family; Shawn Silver and Dutch Touch; Ralph Lauren's Debra Kanibis and Jamie Bahar; and to my Pottery Barn family, who have always been incredibly supportive, encouraging, and so much fun to work with—Cathy Nelson, Sandra Stangl, and Leigh Oshirak, who works harder than anyone I know and still makes me laugh!

A huge thank-you to all the editors and producers that have published my work:

Michael Boodro, Anita Sarsidi, Margaret Russell, Newell Turner, Dara Caponigro, Lisa Newsom, Leslie Rascoe, Deborah Sanders, Deborah Needleman, Sarah Costello, Hamish Bowles, Dana Cowin, Jennifer Smith Hale, Degen Penner, Ann Maine, Pamela Jaccarino, Michelle Adams, Lisa Gregorich, and Sarah Clagett.

Thank you to photographers Miguel Flores-Vianna, Oberto Gili, Victoria Pearson, Roger Davies, Johnny Niccoloro, Mike Gardner, Stephanie Keenan, Jessica Boone, Max Kim Bee, Coliena Rentmeister, Melanie Acevedo, Luca Trovato, Laura Resen, and Joni Noe.

Thanks to my loyal crew at Nathan Turner Inc.: Mai Le, Annabelle Murray, Julie McElvain, Joni Noe, Pamela Brown Kahn, Amanda and Luis Ramos, and Veronica Ayala.

Thanks to my family, whose encouragement and support has always given me the strength to follow my dreams: First and foremost, to my mother and Frank, you gave me the best gift—the freedom and encouragement to seek out my true passions. Without that I would have never ended up selling old furniture! Oh, and sorry about the Amex bills! To my dad, Richard, who taught me the importance of family, and that the best remedy for any problem is a sense of humor. To my brothers Mathew and Chris, thank you for helping me perfect my kitchen skills and for always being willing guinea pigs (remember the cinnamon rolls!). And to my sisters-in-laws, Patti and Jolene, extraordinary mothers who have given me the best gift I could ask for—my nephews and nieces, Lara, Henry, Tommy, William

Henry, and Grace. To my cousin/sister, Stephanie, you started this whole crazy thing with me when it was just you, me, and Daisy in the shop. I can't think of a better beginning. Thank you for always having my back. To all my aunts, uncles, and cousins—you know who you are—all you Turners, O'Dells, Tromanhausers, Lupos and Shallenbergers… Thank you for all the wonderful memories and family traditions that are constant sources of inspiration.

Thanks to all of my friends, who have encouraged and supported my creative endeavors: Jamie Frame, you've witnessed everything since the 6th grade (good thing we're friends or I'd have to kill you!); Mary McDonald/Mums, a true and generous friend; Wendy Walker, because I'm you and you're me; Melissa Metez, aka Cremona, chic and kind—the perfect combo; Janine Corletta/Boots, my fiercely loyal friend; Kay O'Connell, your belief in me has been undying; Janet Crown; Marcia Cross; to "my girls" Minnie Mortimer, Chiara De Rege, Tessa Benson, and Elizabeth Gesas, thank you for always being willing and ready to participate in my shenanigans; Oberto Gili; Miguel Flores-Vianna, thank you for showing me the world through your elegant lens; Milly de Cabrol, Lisa Fine, Charlotte DiCarcaci, Gilles LaGourge, and Yves Gigot for showing me around a kitchen; India Hicks and David Flint Wood, who inspire me by having it all; Carolyne Roehm, a real style icon I've idolized for years; Steve Loguidice; Soledad and Alessandro Twombly, the most talented family I know; Mollie Kelly and Vanessa Martin, my shop "roommates"; Carlota Espinosa, the first person to put me on TV; and Charles Rosasco.

And to my best friend, confidant, and biggest champion, Eric—thank you for being the constant source of love and encouragement that makes all of this possible. Every day I'm amazed by your kindness, generosity, and love, and it's proof that you make my kooky life a better place.

Photo Credits: Pages 4, 5, 8, 22, 26, 28, 29, 32, 34, 35, 36, 37, 40, 41, 42, 43, 44, 45, 59, 60, 62, 63, 65: © Oberto Gili; pages 6, 10, 11, 13, 14, 16, 17, 18, 19, 20, 21, 38, 73, 76, 77, 78, 79, 80, 81, 82, 83, 84, 85, 86, 87, 154, 155, 156, 157, 158, 159, 160, 161, 162, 163, 165, 166, 167, 168, 169, 170, 171, 210, 211, 213, 214, 215: © Miguel Flores-Vianna; pages 24, 25, 143: © Nathan Turner; pages 31, 39, 121: © Joni Noe; pages 46, 47, 48, 49, 50, 51, 53, 54, 56, 57, 172, 173, 174, 175, 176, 177, 178, 179: © Victoria Pearson; pages 66, 67, 68, 69, 114, 115, 116, 117, 119, 120: © Johnny Nicoloro: pages 70, 109, 110, 112, 113: © Max Kim-Bee; pages 74, 88, 89, 90, 91, 92, 93, 95, 96, 97, 202, 203, 204, 206, 207, 208, 209: © Mike Gardner; pages 99, 101, 102, 103, 104, 105, 106, 107: © Coliena Rentmeester; pages 118, 122, 123, 134, 135, 136, 137, 138, 139 © Melanie Acevedo; pages 124, 125, 126, 127, 128, 129, 130, 131, 132, 133: © Roger Davies; pages 140, 144, 146, 147, 148, 149, 150, 151, 152, 153: © Luca Trovato; pages 180, 181, 182, 183, 184, 185, 186, 187, 188, 189, 190, 191: photography by Miguel Flores-Vianna, courtesy of Veranda magazine; pages 193, 194, 195, 196, 197, 198, 199, 201: © Laura Resen; pages 216 (upper left), 217, 218, 220, 221: © Jessica Boone; page 216 (lower right): © Wire Image.

Editor: Rebecca Kaplan

Designer: Erica Heitman-Ford

Production Manager: Kathy Lovisolo

Photo Research: Joni Noe

Library of Congress Cataloging-in-Publication Data

Turner, Nathan.

  Nathan Turner's American style : classic design and effortless entertaining / by Nathan Turner ; introduction by India Hicks.

    pages cm

  ISBN 978-1-4197-0439-0 (hardback)

1. Turner, Nathan—Themes, motives. 2. Interior decoration—United States. 3. Entertaining. I. Title.

NK2004.3.T87A4 2012

747—dc23

           2012020770

Printed and bound in the United States

10 9 8 7 6 5 4 3 2 1

Abrams books are available at special discounts when purchased in quantity for premiums and promotions as well as fundraising or educational use. Special editions can also be created to specification. For details, contact specialsales@abramsbooks.com or the address below.

ABRAMS
THE ART OF BOOKS SINCE 1949

115 West 18th Street

New York, NY 10011

www.abramsbooks.com